Social Media Mai

2019

How Great Marketers Stand Out from the Crowd, Reach Millions of People, and Grow Their Business with Facebook, Twitter, YouTube, and Instagram

and

How You Can Too

Table of Contents

Your Free Gift

As a way of saying thanks for your purchase, I wanted to offer you two free bonuses - ***"The Fastest Way to Make Money with Affiliate Marketing"*** and ***"Top 10 Affiliate Offers to Promote"*** cheat sheets, exclusive to the readers of this book.

To get instant access just go to:

https://theartofmastery.com/chandler-free-gift

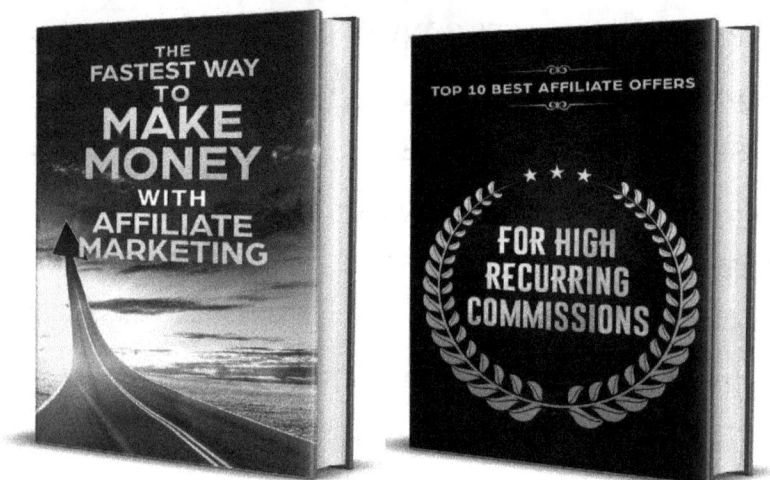

Inside the cheat sheets, you will discover:

- The fastest way to start generating income with affiliate marketing
- My top 10 favorite affiliate offers to promote for high recurring commissions
- Access to a FREE live training where you will learn:
- how one affiliate marketer built a $500,000 a month business all while traveling the world...
- The 3-step system to eliminate risk and instability in your online business
- The 7 biggest mistakes affiliates make in making money online
- How tech companies are giving away <u>FREE MONEY</u> to help you start

And much more...

Introduction

The Age of the Internet is an exciting time to be in. With access to a wealth of information at the palm of the hand and the ability to interact with other people seamlessly across the globe, there is no better time to start a business or maintain one than now.

But with every new era of technology comes a new set of problems that businesses have to regularly face. In this era in particular, there is a strong demand to keep one's offerings relevant and responsive to the time without essentially straying from the business's core goals and vision.

Platforms like YouTube, Facebook, and Instagram offer individuals the opportunity to interact with one another through the creation and sharing of content. For advertisers, this presents an opportunity to directly interact with a new breed of consumers. However, this has its own set of demands as there have been changes in the patterns of consumer behavior brought about by exposure to these new forms of entertainment and communication.

And then there is the matter of how one's own reputation can easily affect the branding of the business online, whether for better or worse. In fact, the high level of interconnectivity and interaction in online communities means that it is easier to inadvertently hurt one's own reputation and harder to repair the same.

Lastly, there is the fact that the rules and standards on how one should create their content and observe proper decorum changes regularly in various social media platforms. What would work a few years ago would be rendered ineffective now and what was deemed acceptable long ago could be seen as offensive and inappropriate by many today.

In essence, managing a business's social media presence as well as extending its reach to new segments of the market is a tightrope walk. You have to balance different demands and standards coming from different social media platforms if you want to funnel quite a lot of traffic to your main webpages and enjoy high customer conversion rates.

But here is a secret: In as much as social media can be intimidating for newcomers, marketing a business here operates roughly on the same principles that make traditional marketing strategies effective. All that is required is to adapt those same principles in one's own social media marketing campaigns.

A deep understanding of the consumer today, with all of their quirks and demands, is necessary in crafting a message that resonates with them the most in every platform that they congregate in. Of course, there is the need to understand what makes each social media platform different from one another and the culture and language that they have adopted for their different communities.

If done right, your business's reputation in the social media world will not only remain favorable to you but will eventually flourish and remain strong for years to come. But, of course, we're getting ahead of ourselves.

It is time now to get acquainted with the intricacies in the field of Social Media Marketing.

Chapter 1: Preliminary Considerations

Before we go through the different social media marketing strategies, we have to address one thing first:

Why is Traditional Marketing Failing?

And to answer this question, we have to understand the basic concept of marketing. In essence, we create advertisements that say something about a business, have it shown in any of the channels we own or pay rent for, and then hope the advertisements draw in enough people willing to become paying customers to your brand.

And so the usual sequence for traditional marketing is always this:

A. Person watches or listens to something.

B. Advertisement butts in for thirty seconds or so to tell the person about what a business is offering.

C. Advertisement ends and the program resumes.

Think of traditional marketing as like a horror movie jump scare. It's something that people more or less do, not expecting to interrupt the mood, and minus the scares.

However, such form of advertising through the different online media right now is suffering from the lowest possible click-through rates and the reason is quite obvious: It's invasive, interruptive, and quite so unpredictable in its appearance that your modern potential customer gets more annoyed than intrigued.

And, given the level of control one person has with the kind of information being fed to them these days, it is not too uncommon for people to tune out from these advertisements as soon as they pop up.

According to surveys, traditional marketing has been rejected by potential audiences in a number of ways, including:

- Teenagers and young adults saying that they would unsubscribe from social media channels and websites if they feature too much forced and un-skippable advertisements.

- 86% of TV viewers immediately changing channels if advertisements start appearing.

- 91% of e-mail subscribers dropping out of their subscriptions in an e-mail list if they receive too many irrelevant notifications.

With such level of discomfort being attributed to traditional forms of advertising done in the online world, it is no surprise why they are not faring well recently.

This implies that you have to create something that would resonate well with your audience the most in any social media channel that you would wish to operate in. This means that you have to mold your message to fit the format and language of every social media site out there.

And to do that, you have to understand what makes for good marketing content.

The Anatomy of Good Advertising Content

Regardless of shape and format, advertising content would always follow the same scheme. In essence, content can come in three major categories which are:

A. **Product** - This is what the advertising is offering to the audience. It is tangible and comes in the form of a purchasable item, service, or other promotion.

B. **Role** - The advertisement basically assumes a role in your audience's life. What is it trying to do for that person? What kind of problems does it solve? What type of questions is it trying to answer? Answering these questions often determines the narrative being presented by your marketing strategies.

C. **Emotion** - An ad of this type is designed to connect to the audience on an emotional, if not personal, level. The point of this content is to evoke some kind of emotional response from your audience. Or, at the very least, it tries to introduce a new kind of perspective that could change the way they regard a certain issue or problem.

So which of these content types are the best for your business? Neither. Each has its own set of strengths and weaknesses which means that focusing on one while disregarding the others is not going to do you any favors in the long run.

For instance, focusing too much on product-based content can make your advertising feel out of touch with your audience, as they don't connect to your brand on a personal level. On the flip side, if you don't have a lot of product-based advertising and too much emotional advertising, then you are not giving your audiences something tangible to anchor their loyalty to your brand.

The anatomy of a highly effective marketing strategy in social media, then, is finding a balance between all three of these categories. Simply put, your marketing must offer something tangible, introduce something that is actionable, plays a relevant role in the lives of your target audience, and can connect to them on a personal level.

Organic and Paid Marketing: Which is Which?

A common misconception with marketing is that all types of marketing content can be lumped into a single category. The truth, however, is that marketing can fall into two categories: organic and paid.

A smart business owner would use both advertising types in tandem to reach their target market and even discover new segments in the process. However, in order to do that, you have to understand what makes both advertising types different from one another.

Organic Marketing

Marketing falling under this category is best for a number of functions including:

- Establishing the style and voice of your brand.

- Educating potential audiences.

- Driving traffic to landing pages.

- Making the business an authority in a certain topic or industry.

Simply put, organic marketing is there to increase the "awareness" for your business. The cycle of organic marketing often follows the same sequence which is:

A. The scheduled production and publishing of content like blog posts and articles for Search Engine Optimization (SEO) purposes. The articles must be aligned to what your target market cares for the most, the problems that they face, and even issues that are being tackled in the wider industry that your business is a part of.

B. Sharing of these posts on social media. Again, the way that this content is shared must be in line with the format and language of that platform.

C. Tagging influencers and other appropriate brands in your social media posts as well as using your content in regular newsletters for subscribers.

D. Monitoring how the content is being consumed by the market. Analytics and other monitoring tools will become crucial in this phase, as it tells you whether or not people are engaging with your content and if your content is funneling traffic from your social media accounts to your main web pages.

If it is not obvious to you, organic marketing is focused on tactics that produce authentic and value-based reactions. In essence, if you produce something of value to your audience, you are convincing them more to convert into paying customers. And if you already have converted them into paying customers, the content you further produce will help in ensuring that they remain loyal to your business.

Paid Marketing

On the other hand, paid marketing is designed to help businesses optimize the sales conversion process. If organic marketing is there to "establish" your presence, then paid marketing is there to "push" it. Due to this, paid marketing is much more focused on sales and generating a purchase-focused action among target audiences.

How the paid marketing cycle goes is as follows:

A. Commissioning for the Creation of "Advertising Content." This would also include creating a schedule of when these ads are going to be published and in what sets.

B. Once the initial results are in for every published set, the marketing team then reviews which ads performed the best. Some would even invest more money in improving these top-performing ads or creating new ads similar to them.

C. Once every quarter is complete, the marketing team then reviews data drawn from the entire marketing campaign. Things to look for are expenses, returns of investment, returns on assets, and other important metrics.

The key to success with paid marketing is to be specific with your goals in order to produce specific actions. For instance, each paid ad might be linked to a very specific page of your website such as the landing page, the sales page, or the products page.

Other specific actions you could drive with paid advertising includes:

- Improving returns on investment and assets.
- Making a specific impression on the various platforms you operate in.
- Hitting specific sales goals or, better yet, going beyond them.
- Optimizing ads in real-time.

- Testing marketing campaigns before full implementation to identify what parts make them effective (and where they might fail).

*However, the most **important** metrics you have to look out for in paid advertising will include:*

A. **Conversion Rates** - The traffic coming from your social media pages that not only engage with your web pages but would actually complete the sales conversion process (more on this later).

B. **Engagement** - The amount of likes, shares, views, and comments that each ad generates in a period of time after being published.

C. **Advertisement Type** - The types of advertisements that had the highest rates in conversion and engagement.

Where do These Advertising Types Fit in Your Marketing Campaign?

The one thing that you have to understand is that both paid and organic marketing actually complement each other well. There are even certain aspects where both advertisement types overlap into each other which can optimize conversion rates and incoming traffic in your main web pages.

However, the truth is that both advertisement forms are rarely used in tandem due to budget concerns. Paid advertising, as the name implies, requires you to invest more in order to generate tangible results.

On the other hand, even if you have a large advertising budget, you are not going to improve on your business's sales conversion if your content does not naturally engage with your target audience.

As such, it is important that you identify where you must use paid and organic marketing either in tandem or exclusively. Some of your marketing goals will rely on one form while others can be achieved if you used either type.

Once you have found a balance between paid and organic marketing, what you must do then is to constantly test and improve on your strategies throughout the entire campaign.

Some (Harsh) Social Media Realities That You Must Face

What you have to understand is that changes in consumer behavior has not only affected traditional marketing, but even online marketing. What worked for social media sites a few years back no longer applies today.

As such, if you want to truly survive in the world of social media, you need to face some realities about the current state of affairs.

Reality #1: Brand Recognition No Longer Means as Much as It Did

Traditional marketing has always been the act of telling the rest of the world that your business is the best of whatever it is doing or, at the very least, a fairly trusted brand in the field. But how does the rest of the social media market treat that same line whenever a company says it today? Noise. Loud, unnecessary, irrelevant noise.

The harshest truth you might face with social media is that nobody on there really cares about your business. And those that swear that they support your business won't be there for long if you start making mistakes here and there.

So, if the image you create is no longer important, what then matters for social media people? The answer is one word: solutions.

Simply put, marketing today is no longer about how well-known or trusted your brand is, but how applicable your offerings are in solving actual problems. As such, those that offer the best possible solutions to a problem, and at reasonable prices, tend to be at the top.

Reality #2: It's a Free-For-All

A few years back, the only kind of competition you needed to worry about came from the companies that offered the same products/services as you, or those that targeted the same demographics. Today, competition can come in any form or size.

In most cases, the competition you should take seriously today will come from smaller companies or lesser-known people. The reason for this is that they are closer to their target markets and can keep them engaged through a mixture of organic and paid marketing schemes (more so in the former).

In fact, you will find that less popular brands and individuals can garner stronger followings while big companies like Gap, Pepsi, and Spirit Airlines have to deal with backlash after backlash from their tone deaf social media strategies.

Also, the increase of volume in competition today gives rise to the problem of information overload for target markets. The more manufactured noise that similar companies generate on social media, the more people tend to ignore what they are trying to say.

Reality #3: Philanthropy is the New Form of Marketing

In a rather odd turn of events, marketing today has taken a rather altruistic tone. And no, this does not mean that companies have forgotten that they are capitalists by heart, as they still aim to make a lot of money from the markets.

What the shift means is that more and more people respond to marketing strategies that make them feel good. And what makes people feel good right now is if companies "stand up" for the "little man."

As such, you might notice that some companies are beginning to take up a stance in social issues, political topics, and even environmental concerns. By showing that they care for the rest of the world, companies give potential customers some value of sorts.

However, there is the drawback of becoming too political or ideological with your marketing. What you have to remember is that people don't like being talked down to. Whether it is you telling them how to live or making them feel ashamed for not caring too much, you can expect a lot of blowback from the market if the message you think is noble is perceived to be pushy and abrasive.

And there are quite a lot of brands out there that overdo it with taking a stand on social issues. The key to success, then, is to temper a business's newfound altruistic side with the notion that one is in business to give people what they want.

Either way, the point is that your brand has to give something of value if you want potential customers to trust it. Otherwise, you are not going to be as relevant in the years to come which, in turn, affects your visibility in the social media arena.

What this all means is that your marketing strategies in social media are utterly dependent on how people behave on them, whether you like it or not. And understanding the behavior of the modern day potential customer is crucial for the sole reason that, in order for your strategies to be deemed successful in social media, they must complete a step-by-step process of becoming paying customers.

Chapter 2: The Sales Conversion Process

Although marketing might sound complicated, it actually follows a rather simple and straightforward sequence. Here's the catch, though: Any member of your audience could be in either of these stages currently.

The 4 Stages: How a Prospect Becomes a Paying Customer

You have to know in what stage of the conversion process your audience is in to craft a message that would resonate with them well. So, how does one person go from an absolute stranger to your business to a loyal customer?

They do so in 4 steps.

1. *Attraction*

Since this is the start of the process, you can expect it to be the more labor-intensive phase compared to subsequent ones. This is where any business would have to introduce people to their products/services and give them the assurance that whatever they are paying for is good.

Of course, since this is the start of the process, the target audience at this phase absolutely does not know anything about the business. As such, the goal here is to inform and educate them by answering their queries. Visibility is a major factor in this phase which is why it is recommended that you adopt a rather aggressive strategy, especially if your business is relatively new to the world of social media.

2. *Conversion*

Once your social media pages are funneling traffic to your web pages, the focus shifts from introducing them to the brand to turning them into potential leads. Here, you may have to rely on your web pages' design and even the presentation of your content to give the push that your leads need to complete the conversion process. You should also have set up systems in your pages where you can easily retarget these people at a later date.

However, your social media pages will still play a crucial role in this part. Through your channels, you can offer them something of value like discounts and promises of access to high-end content if they subscribe or register to your brand.

However, don't go straight for a "hard sell" by immediately offering them all of your available products or services, as you want them to get to know your business more first.

In other words, the goal here is to entice the leads so they would stay on your pages long enough, and make them trust you to the point that they will trade their basic information for something that they can find value with.

3. *Closing*

Once you have your leads, the goal then is to turn these people into paying customers. Since you already have their basic information, retargeting your leads should be fairly straightforward now. Once you have a pool of potential leads to your site via those subscriptions to your social media profiles, you can provide them with even better offers so they would initiate the sales process.

This can be the most demanding part of the sales conversion cycle as you are now aiming to convince people to part with their money to try out something that you are offering. The chances of people bailing on the process is quite high at this part but those that are sufficiently convinced with your marketing at this point will have increased chances of closing a deal with you.

At this point, you can only rely on the quality of your marketing strategies in the first two phases as well as the ones you are publishing at this phase. If they are quite good, people will not only initiate a transaction with the business but would actually go through the entire process, resulting in a sale.

4. *Delighting*

Most business are content with turning one visitor into a paying customer. After all, the sales conversion process is technically complete. However, it would be better if you maintain a relationship with satisfied customers.

Once the main sales process is complete, the next phase will involve enticing these customers with even more offers. The goal for your marketing at this point is to give people a reason to come back to your channels.

The reason for this is quite simple: There is no better endorser to your business than people who actually tried your offerings and found them to be good. If all of your subsequent offerings live up to the promises in your marketing, you can establish a loyal customer base which will promote your business for you in their own little ways.

Nurturing Your Leads

Let's assume that you mastered the art of converting strangers into loyal customers and you know of strategies that can quickly drum up interest for your brand. So now, you have quite a lot of traffic going from your social media pages to your main website.

However, there is still one problem that you would have to face: Not all of those visitors actually become customers. In fact, the people that actually convert into customers coming from your social media pages don't even comprise 20% of your site's day-to-day traffic.

So why aren't visitors actually making important purchasing decisions when on your social media pages? The answer is simple:

Not Everyone Who Clicks Through Your Content is Ready to Make a Purchase

You could focus on generating leads all you want. But if you want to see noticeable changes in your traffic and conversion rates, you'll have to nurture your potential leads.

One key aspect here is that you must understand that each potential lead has their own story to tell. As such, they should be handled in different ways to make them convert into customers and then free promoters.

To perform lead nurturing properly, there are a few things that you have to keep in mind:

1. *Know What They Need*

As was stated, not every lead is the same. Because of this, your business has to directly interact with them to understand in what phase of the conversion process they currently fall into. Have they just discovered your business? From what social media pages did they come from? Have they filled out one of your forms or subscribed to one of your channels?

Knowing where they currently are in the conversion process will give you an idea if they are ready to try out what you are offering or not. However, just remember that just because a lead is not yet ready to make that final step towards conversion now does not mean that they won't do so in the near future.

2. *Communicate*

Once you know what they need, you then need to build a relationship with them. And just like in the real world, you can build trust with complete strangers if you initiate a conversion with them. Don't worry, though. These people are already subscribed to you so you should have no problems contacting them later on.

Having a direct conversation with your audience will actually help you appear sincere and genuine. You have to keep in mind that people today know if the "person" they are talking to online is an actual human being or is a program using a generic comment to get them to talk.

As such, you should learn how to personalize the content your business publishes on social media to build trust with your audience. The more your humanity shines through your social media content, the more people will give attention to you.

3. *Mind the Frequency and the Approach*

One surefire way to scare off a lot of leads from your business is if you are perceived as pushy. Leads often tune out any kind of content that immediately sells them stuff and appears more than once in a day. Remember that marketing that relies heavily on spamming your message is going to infuriate a lot of people these days in social media.

If possible, limit your engagements with your leads to once or twice every week. Also, you have to have your content marketing designed to follow the sales conversion process. Stage 1 of the process might require content with informative tones while stages 2, 3, and 4 can go for a more promotional tone.

The point is that you should never drive your leads crazy with too much promotions that they would be turned off if they encounter your brand later on.

4. *Mold Your Message to the Platform*

The notion that there is more than one way to say a message is still applicable in the world of social media. When nurturing your leads, you have to adapt to how they speak and interact with each other depending on which social media site they usually hang out on.

What you have to remember is that each social media site acts as its own community with its set of guidelines and culture. And within the larger community lies smaller communities from where you can find specific customer personalities.

For instance, people coming from Instagram need to be reached out to in a visually-focused way while those from Facebook and Twitter need you to constantly interact with them through comments and the sharing of content.

Again, this all boils down to helping people see that there is someone operating that social media profile. And if they know that they are dealing with an actual human being at the other end of the line, they are more than willing to start a conversation with the business.

Granted, understanding the conversion process does not ensure that more people are going to respond well to your marketing strategies. However, what it does do is that it helps you understand that every potential lead needs to be approached in a manner that is unique and, more importantly, personal.

Why is this so? It's because intimacy is actually quite important in the world of social media. Regardless of whether that person uses Facebook or Twitter or YouTube, they are looking for an anchor from which they can connect to brands online on a personal level. And if you can provide that, then you have established a relationship with that person that ensures profit on your side and value on the other.

And, with that done, it is time to venture into the weird, wild world of social media.

Chapter 3: Marketing on Facebook Part I: Benefits and Successful Strategies

Arguably the largest social media platform currently on the Internet, Facebook, is used by an estimated 19 billion users—with 2.38 billion from 2018 alone. This is approximately 8% more than what statistics showed the previous year.

A highly diverse social media site, Facebook, can be used for a number of applications and can cater to a vast range of people. Whether you are a highly political activist in Malaysia or a budding entrepreneur in Romania, there's always something for everyone when they log in to Facebook.

Given its strong staying power and wide reach, it's hard to comprehend that Facebook merely started as a small program between friends at Harvard. And perhaps due to its wide reach, one can see quite a lot of potential from marketing their business here.

But before we go about learning how to do marketing on Facebook effectively, we have to address one question first:

What's in It For Businesses If They Market on Facebook Primarily?

To answer that question, let us look at six key benefits that the site offers.

1. Massive Exposure

As was stated, there are more than a billion people actively using Facebook across the world on any given day. Sure, there are some countries where Facebook is not as popular due to local alternatives, but the reach of the platform remains on a global scale.

This means that exposure for your business is also on a global scale. If you post something, and your profile's setting has all posts set to "Public," absolutely everyone can see your post in their news feed.

Of course, there are settings placed by the site so that not every public post would appear in your news feed. This prevents users from having to scroll through tons of posts from total strangers just to see what their friends are posting. However, the potential for global scale exposure for your marketing is still there.

And to make sure that the reach of your marketing is wide, Facebook offers several marketing platforms for businesses. This comes in the form of pages, groups, and your conventional online advertising channels.

For instance, your business can create a group page where you can promote community activities. Other people can then join in on this group and post their thoughts and ideas. With just one page, you can promote and interact with your potential customers regardless of where they are located currently.

And aside from these channels, Facebook does allow businesses to target specific demographics within the platform. Since people enter in information when registering to the site, the website then groups these people according to what they like according to their profile info.

One neat example of this would be Dove's campaign in 2013 called "Real Beauty Sketches." Featuring people getting their faces drawn by professional sketch artists, this campaign showed that people were rather overly critical on how they described themselves versus how other people actually describe them.

Apparently, that hit a nerve in a lot of people coming from a number of demographics (some of which did not even belong to Dove's target segments). And, as a result, the video received more than 100,000 comments and 6.3 million shares within two weeks after it was published.

And the best part about this is that Facebook's current design allows for content to "go viral" quickly (more on this later on). Recently, Facebook's algorithms can even predict what a user likes and auto-recommend several brands for them.

All it takes is for businesses to publish something good and for it to reach the right amount of people within a short time.

2. *Targeting Accuracy*

Facebook's current layout allows for businesses to target very specific people based on their interests. How they manage to get ahold of this information from people is actually quite ingenious. When a person registers to the site, they are recommended to list down the things that they like and what they are interested in.

Also, people have a tendency to create patterns when they interact with other pages on the site. In essence, every content you share on Facebook, along with the pages that you like and followe, and even the type of pages that you comment in, create a "profile" which allows you to be categorized under several demographics.

This profile, in turn, will be used by business owners to target specific people on the platform. For example, if your brand caters to young adults with some form of financial independence, you could choose several demographic options within Facebook when posting content. This include options like ages below 35, residing in metropolitan cities, and sharing interest in subjects like marketing, business, and careers.

The number of demographic options available on Facebook allows businesses to mix and match customer profiles to target multiple segments at once.

For instance, Ben and Jerry's could target men and women under the age of 40 with an interest in desserts for their ads. Or Victoria's Secret could target women ages 30 to 50 with an interest in fashion. Either way, you can be certain that your content will reach the right kind of people after you publish it.

Aside from targeting, Facebook also allows businesses to accurately retarget past customers. This is because their algorithm also looks into the interaction that people make with your main page.

So, in practice, Facebook allows businesses to automatically update past customers with new offerings and content without having to tediously build something like an e-mail subscription list.

3. *Cost Effectiveness*

The beauty with Facebook is that it can serve as your main website and official marketing channel. In fact, many small businesses (since they don't have the budget to set up a website) make their Facebook profiles their official business page.

Of course, there are the ad options which allow you to target potential segments of the market using information that Facebook has already gathered for you. Posting a paid ad on Facebook is going to cost you but the prices remain budget-friendly regardless of the size and reach of your business.

How Facebook charges you per ad can be done in a number of ways. The most popular of these are the **Cost Per Million** and **Cost Per Click** systems. Basically, you will pay for your ads by the exposure they get and not from the ad space you are renting (unlike in TV and radio).

The more engagements your ads generate and the click-through rate is high without people abandoning the ad as it is being shown, the more you will have to pay for them.

However, there are even cheaper payment methods available for businesses. There is the **Optimized Cost Per Million** rate where the site charges you based on the number of people coming from only the target demographic you have set for the ad.

The next option is the **Cost Per Action** scheme where you are charged only if people perform the specific set of actions after encountering your ad on their news feed. This includes liking your page or sharing the content you have just posted.

And if that is not enough, Facebook allows users to set the daily limit for their ad expenses. Of course, you can adjust the settings if you feel that your campaigns are not reaching the expected amount of people you are expecting. This way, you won't overspend for your Facebook marketing campaigns.

4. *Organic Brand Awareness (and Loyalty)*

Facebook encourages profile holders to directly interact with one another, regardless if that user is a private individual or a company. This direct line of interaction means that you can provide fast customer support which, on paper, should help in increasing awareness and loyalty to your brand.

What you have to understand is that more and more people are relying on Facebook now when making purchasing decisions. For instance, one person might be looking for a set of clothes that your business can supply.

To decide whether or not to do business with you, they look at your profile to see how quickly you can respond to queries. They want to know if you have been directly interacting with your customers, as this is a telltale sign that you can provide what they are looking for in the fastest time possible.

Engagement in Facebook is done through comments, private messages, and the content being published and shared on your page. And this, in turn, can lead to stronger connections with your prospective leads. Of course, a stronger connection increases the chances of conversion.

One other thing to consider here is that Facebook customers can make or break your reputation there. Users can place reviews and ratings on business pages which tells prospective customers how good (or bad) that business is to deal with.

And, also, people can tag in their own statuses. Whether that status is disparaging or praising your business, the reach of word of mouth on Facebook is quite wide and that could affect your brand in more ways than one.

5. *Funneling Web Traffic*

Integrating Facebook to your main online marketing campaign is easy. If linked properly, the Facebook profile for your business can be linked to your main website. If you think that making people go to another site can turn off potential leads, the truth is it doesn't.

What you have to remember is that people who click on any link that you provide do so willingly for 90% of the time. As such, they are more receptive to what you have to offer if they came first from your Facebook profile.

Once they are on your landing page, you can immediately shift to the third phase of the conversion process: Enticing them with offers that would make them start a transaction with you. As such, you can expose them to more direct calls to action or recommend they take a look at your products or services page.

6. *Insights*

The best advantage that Facebook gives to businesses is the ability to gauge how their content is being received in real time. The page of a business profile usually gives its users important information such as the number of likes for the page, engagement for each particular content, and the people who engaged with posts. All of that information is readily available when you click on their respective tabs.

This is quite unlike traditional marketing where you have to pay someone to get the data you need to improve on your marketing. And by the time you have received that data, there is a chance that response to your marketing campaign has changed again, rendering the data irrelevant.

Aside from on-page metrics, Facebook also has the Adverts Manager feature which lets business track how their advertisements are performing in the platform. The Adverts Manager can provide a number of valuable data including:

- Impressions - The number of times a single ad was shown.

- Reach - The number of people who saw the ad.

- Frequency - The number of people who visited your business page through the ad.

- Engagement - The number of times specific actions were done on your page by visitors. This includes liking the page or its posts, commenting on posts, and sharing content.

Granted, the data being shown to you will require an appreciation on the technical aspects of marketing in order to be valuable to you. However, Facebook does present the information to business owners in a manner simple enough that even those with no understanding of analytics could get the gist behind the figures.

The best part about Facebook's Insights feature is that it is completely compatible with the language used by Google's Analytics system. Using both, you can get an idea as to how your Facebook customer base is performing in relation to the wider marketing campaign you have implemented for the rest of the Internet.

7. *Boosting SEO*

The Search Engine Optimization (SEO) serves as the core of many marketing campaigns used currently. After all, marketing is about improving on your visibility and this is often made certain if your pages appear on the topmost results in the Search Engine Results Pages (SERPs).

This can be done naturally by having a key understanding of how search engine bots come up with their rankings for results. Basically, a search engine scours the entire Internet for information that would answer a query made in the search box.

So, if somebody is looking for Japanese restaurants in Los Angeles, the search engine would immediately look for pages that showcase the best places in that city where you could find that kind of food.

Facebook, in recent years, has been optimizing their layout so that their links would show up on Page 1 of the SERPs. If you were to look for your business pages in Google, chances are that your Facebook profile would come out in the top ten results on the first page.

This is good if people already know about your business's name. But what if they don't? Provided that you are constantly publishing content that people engage with on Facebook, the search engine bots might start noticing your page more and will give it a better ranking in queries that may not contain your name but definitely contain questions that your business might answer.

8. *Becoming Mobile Ready*

As of now, 60% of users on Facebook access the platform via their mobile devices. And as this percentage continues to grow, it becomes more important for your business to become optimized for mobile devices.

Remember that the navigation style for either desktop and mobile platforms are substantially different. Some sites are optimized for desktop, which means they are great to go through on a PC but are absolutely frustrating to do so on a mobile. As such, a good business owners needs to have their websites optimized for all types of devices and navigation schemes.

A good thing about Facebook is that it has been optimized for mobile devices. Your business page on the site is easy to access for both PC and mobile users. In fact, the mobile version might be friendlier for users as the most important information on your website is all placed up front. This includes:

- The hours that you are open for business (according to your time zone, of course).

- Your address.

- The reviews your pages get, along with some ratings.

- Phone number and other contact details.

- Your most recent posts.

The only drawback with the mobile version is for your part as the owner. The Custom Apps tab does not appear on the mobile unless you have the proper apps, like ShortStack, or access the site via mobile browsers that have the settings that allow the sites to be viewed via their desktop layout.

This means that monitoring your advertisement's performance through a mobile device is not as effective compared to the desktop.

9. *Monitoring the Competition*

One of Facebook's newest features for businesses is the ability to identify competitors within a specific area. Just below a business's page lies a tab that says "Pages to Watch."

If you click on the "+Add 5 Pages" option, you will be taken to another box which lists other businesses similar to yours operating in the same area as you.

And aside from informing you of your competitors, this feature also displays how these businesses are faring as far as their advertising is concerned.

And if you are wondering why this is quite useful, think of it this way:

Every business in the past has always wondered how their competition is faring in real time. If one of their advertisements was well-liked, a competitor would definitely want to know the figures that would show how effective that piece of marketing was.

It's even been a practice in companies in the past few decades to send "agents" as employees in rival companies just so that they could get hold of that company's advertising and sales figures.

So, if a new business page just popped up, you would want to know if their marketing strategies are effective. Things such as Likes, Comments, and Shares can tell you if that business is resonating with the local market which, of course, gives you an idea as to how to improve on your own marketing campaigns.

It is a bit like corporate espionage but perfectly discreet and legit.

Effective Facebook Marketing Strategies

So far we've only covered why Facebook is a great place to do your marketing at. However, we have yet to fully discuss how to effectively market your business on the platform.

So how does one go about doing that? Remember that there is hard and fast rule on doing your marketing on Facebook. However, there have been trends and tricks used by businesses in the past that allowed for a growth in their presence on the platform. Here are some of them:

1. Review Sharing

One of the best ways to stand out from the crowd on Facebook is something called "social proof." Basically, if your business can prove that what you say is true, people will trust it more.

That kind of proof, however, is not something that you can produce on your own. It only comes from people who are at the receiving end of what you offer: your customers.

This is where *review sharing* comes into play and you can implement it in two steps. First, you request that all your customers leave a comment on your business page. You can even offer an incentive for those that do leave their reviews, such as codes for discounts at your main website or a freebie that comes in their next order.

Once you have enough positive reviews, you must then take a screenshot of a review and post it as an image in your next status update. Don't forget to tag that customer and give them a sincere *thank you* for the review.

You can also use reviews coming from others sites like Google+ and Yelp. E-mails coming from satisfied customers also work, although you might have to ask permission from them before you post them.

And if reviews come few and far between, you can always use a customer's post regarding their experience with you. That works as social proof as well.

2. *Groups*

There are a number of benefits to expect from creating a Facebook group. This includes:

● More direct line of customer service.

● Multiple networking opportunities.

- Putting all your customer base on a single, well-connected community.

- Creating a list of products that you have currently available.

The beauty with groups is that you can give your customers a community where they can share thoughts and ideas with you having full control over the conversations as the administrator.

And since groups are comprised of people with similar interests, you can have your group focus itself on any subject that you will dictate when creating it.

For instance, if you are the owner of a scale model shop, you can create a group on Facebook for people who are interested in scale modeling. To keep the group alive, you might post some content like tips on how to build scale models or on repairing damages while also allowing community members to share their ideas and builds.

Once the group has reached a level of activity, it becomes its own self-sustaining community. This will open your business to more opportunities to market like local events and group meets (more on these later on).

An administrator, of course, has the added responsibility of controlling the behavior of group members and the content being shared there. You can approve or reject posts, add, block or reject members, and direct the flow of communication in every thread that is started in the community.

Handling a Facebook group can get demanding at times but you can be certain that the community you build will have a strong connection with your business in the years to come. That is, of course, if you constantly interact with the rest of the community and maintain a favorable relationship with them.

3. *Events*

Supposed that your business has some major event on the weekend like, say, an anniversary or a famous person is going to visit it. You can use Facebook to notify the rest of the world of what is going to happen with your business through the Events feature.

Creating an event on Facebook is rather simple. You only need to go to the Events tab and select the Create Event option. You will then be transferred to a box where you will fill in details like:

- The date and time
- The category of the event
- Event keywords
- Link to important websites for tickets or for more information

You can also add in a photo for the event like an official banner or any promotion related to it.

Once you have created the event, Facebook will do the rest to inform other people within your target demographics and your customers about it. People can even choose to respond to the notification by declaring their intent to go there.

Aside from Facebook doing the heavy work of promoting your event, you can also do things that will make sure that everybody else will know about it.

A. Add Directions - You'd want those people who have shown interest for your event to get there on time. Giving directions to your place tends to do just that.

B. Invite - Use your friends list to promote the event. Facebook allows you to manually invite people you know to an event. Once invited, they will be given regular reminders of the event until the day arrives.

C. Promote - Dedicate a post on your page everyday about the upcoming event. This way, those that have yet to be made aware of your event will be informed. However, do this promotion no more than three times per day. After all, you don't want to spam your message, as too much of this can turn off would-be-goers.

4. *Go Local*

If there's one thing that has always been consistent with Facebook, it is that people there love to celebrate things that are part of their local identity. You can use this to your advantage by coming up with content that celebrates every local landmark or any other noteworthy object in your area.

To do this, plan to publish content on your Facebook page that tackles your local culture. For instance, if you live in Idaho, you may link an article there that talks about all the weird stories coming from this region.

If your business offers events management services, you might publish articles about the upcoming events in your area. Or, if you are a restaurant, you might want to publish an article that highlights your city's local delicacies.

Giving your content a strong connection to your local culture would make it unique when compared to your competitors. Plus, people on Facebook love to share articles, especially those that cover things that have a personal connection with them.

5. *Tag*

To quickly build traction on Facebook, you can tag popular people, businesses, and other pages that share your interest in each post. For instance, if your post is about an upcoming event in your local area, you can tag the people that are coming there in your posts or you can name-drop whoever is going to make an appearance there.

Tagging is one way of quickly inserting yourself in a larger, ongoing conversation in your local area's social media circle. And, in line with the *going local* strategy, tagging is one way of increasing hype for an upcoming event, which also increases your prospects of entering into collaborations with other businesses.

Puma, for instance, is quite known for their aggressive social media marketing strategies. If they are sponsored in an upcoming athletic event, you can be certain that their official Facebook page will churn out content that promotes the event to the local people on a daily basis.

Also, you can tag upcoming local events to your posts. If you are helping set up a concert, tag that event. If you are manning a booth at a local convention for gamers and nerds, tag that event. If your Facebook group met each other in the real world for a round of drinks or dinner, post that meetup on your page.

The goal here is to give an impression that your business is actively networking itself to the local community. Showing earnest effort in making your business visible and relevant in the local area tends to resonate with a lot of potential customers, especially those that live and work near your place of business.

Warning: Tagging might be an effective marketing tool but it is also one strategy that could be disastrous for you if overdone. If you start tagging pages and other businesses in your post even if they have nothing to do with whatever your status update contains, chances are you are going to out yourself as a spam page. And if people see you as a spammer, they will immediately turn off your ads whenever they see it in their feeds.

As such, pick and choose whoever you are going to tag in your posts carefully. Pick the ones who are quite relevant to your status update and would provide the most impact with your audience.

6. *Scheduling Your Posts*

This might sound elementary, but you should be consistent with your posts. Constant activity does increase your visibility which brings attention to your page. And with attention comes engagements, and Facebook's algorithms do pick up on pages where people go to frequently.

Your posts should target a specific demographic by focusing on a central subject. Also, it should have the aim to either inform, entertain, or empower your audience.

So what are the best days to post something on your page? If you want to know that, head to your Insights page and go to the Posts tab.

There, you will be given the option to schedule your posts. If you hover over the day portion, you will be able to see the hours where people visit your site the most.

Aside from this, you can also use apps like HootSuite and Sprout Special to understand what type of content resonates with your audience the most. These apps can provide you with metrics and other information on which types of content have been liked and shared the most on your Facebook page.

On your part, you can also find ways to improve the presentation of your posts. As such, here are a few things to consider before you post a status update.

- **Use Emoticons Smartly** - For some reason, posts that use emoticons get commented at 33% and get shared 57% more times than posts that use bare text. However, you should find a balance between emoticons and text, as a focus on the former makes your status a bit hard to read through.

If possible, always put more focus on your text with the emoticons used only to enhance any point you want to get across.

- **Be Inquisitive** - Any post that takes the form of a question gets better engagement through comments. The reason is simple, a question is actionable by nature. It subtly encourages people to do something by satisfying the query it presents.

You can also use polls as an alternative to basic questions. The point is that any post that demands an answer tends to start a conversation, and conversations are one strong form of engagement on Facebook.

7. *Create a Contest*

Studies have shown that Facebook users love two things the most: participation and free stuff. This is where a contest comes into play, as it gives people the chance to enjoy both.

Setting up a contest on Facebook is not as hard as you think. For instance, your page might have this cool or weird picture and you want its engagement to increase. What you can do with that picture is share it with a "Caption This" status update.

Soon enough, your post should get more than a handful of comments if your audience base is quite large. Of course, you should offer something in return for all those people that commented something.

If your business is selling some products, you might offer one item for free. If you are running a service-based business, perhaps a discount on your service fees or a free consultation period could serve as a prize.

Then, you can promote this contest also through the Events tab or through your group. This way, your content gets shown frequently in the news feed of other users which should drive traffic to your page.

However, Facebook does have rules for anyone who wishes to hold a contest there. Before you set up one, you must know what you can't do. They include:

- Requiring contestants share your page or post or write something on your timeline.
- Requiring contestants to like YOUR page to enter.
- Requiring contestants to tag themselves in your post or image to enter.

There are several more things that you can't do for contests as listed out in Facebook's Community Guidelines page. Just make sure that you are quite aware of what Facebook deems acceptable for events so they won't shut your contest down.

8. *Improving "Foot Traffic"*

After all is said and done, you would want your Facebook followers to actually convert into paying customers. Sadly, this is where a lot of businesses are experiencing difficulties with.

You have to think of your Facebook profile as like a marketing email and your physical store as your website's sales page. In order to increase foot traffic, the path that turns digital engagements into real-world sales, you have to have a message that is compelling enough to make readers perform a specific action. This should be then partnered with, and to quote Don Vito Corleone of the *Godfather* saga, "An offer that they can't refuse."

There are ways that can encourage people to come into your store if they encountered your Facebook page. This includes, but is not limited to, the following:

- Creating a poll centered on your products and their uses.
- Run in-store events regularly and promote them on Facebook.
- Promote coupons that people can use in your store.

- Turning your Facebook page into an online shop or have it directly linked to your main website's sales page.

- Align your businesses with causes and charities that people care about in recent times.

In Summary:

Executing marketing tactics on Facebook will require constant experimentation. You have to always remember that even the best designed message might not be received by the public in a manner that you have expected.

Also, what works (and doesn't) for other businesses might not apply to yours. Take the time to understand how your audience behaves and what Facebook deems to be acceptable. This is because Facebook, like any other social media platform, tends to change the rules from time to time.

Chapter 4: Marketing on Facebook Part II: Creating Your Own Marketing Campaign and Success Stories

Facebook, like any other website out there, wants to remain competitive. And to remain competitive, they must constantly reinvent themselves, which includes changing the rules for users.

In the early 2000s, the team at Facebook found out that a major percentage of their user base included business entities that wanted to reach out to a wider market. From small businesses to large corporate behemoths, every business out there wants a place on Facebook where they can discover a new community to turn into customers.

This has led to Facebook introducing some changes that were specifically meant for marketing a business. And whether these changes hurt or help your wider online marketing campaign is something that you must decide for yourself.

Crucial Components

So, this does give rise to the question: What has changed with Facebook? Here are some that you should pay attention to, as they involve the marketing aspects of your Facebook page.

1. *Customizable Audience Requirements*

Since July of 2018, Facebook has introduced new requirements when targeting custom audiences that were organized through customer files. In essence, when you collect information from Facebook for your marketing campaign, there are three new options made available for you. These include:

- Directly from Customers

- Directly from Partners

- Customers and Partners

How this change affects advertising is quite considerable. Whenever a user clicks on the "Why Am I Seeing This?" button on an ad, they would see how that business got ahold of their information. This would give power to the user to tune out any advertising that they don't like especially if they feel that that business got ahold of their information without their consent.

For businesses, however, this means that they must rely on the Business Manager feature to an even greater degree and must agree to newer terms in the Custom Audience tab if they want to get ahold of valuable user information.

2. *Power to the Audience*

Aside from flagging down business pages that got ahold of their information without their consent, customers are now given more options by Facebook to directly dictate the effectiveness of their advertising on the site. This can be done through the eCommerce Review tool which allows users to leave a rating on the business page after every transaction.

Although the Review feature is not something that is not exactly new to Facebook, the changes in it will help or hurt your advertising depending on the rating. If the ratings on the page are generally good, Facebook's algorithm will allow for your ads to show more in the news feeds of users.

If you start getting a few negative comments, Facebook will give you a notification informing you of such. Of course, as any smart business owner, you should take the notification as a reminder to improve on your services.

If, however, the negative reviews outweigh your positive ones to a considerable degree, you will find that the reach of your ads will be severely limited and the type of content you can publish will be restricted. Worse, Facebook might outright ban you if your page gets more than a handful of community strikes.

Just keep in mind that not every customer experience is going to be great. Some will give you glowing reviews and some will leave poor ones. This means that Facebook won't penalize you for one bad review over a hundred good ones. The restrictions only apply if Facebook notices a recurring pattern in the overall experience you give to your users.

3. *Other Algorithm Changes*

As of now, Facebook is still using the 5 Star scheme for their reviews. It's a fairly dependable system but it is quite notorious for resulting in massive shifts in the overall rating. For instance, if you get 2 to 3 star reviews, the overall rating for your business could change by several points and decimals even if you have 100 4 to 5 star reviews.

Facebook understands this and has been finding ways to make reviews even more reliable than what the number rating would imply. The review algorithm would now detect key phrases and words being left in your reviews as well as the testimonials and recommendations made by your customers.

As a matter of fact, scores right now would say something like "Based on the opinion of XXX people" or "Recommended by XXX people."

The implication for this is that Facebook will make sure that businesses that constantly provide good customer experiences will have better ratings even with the presence of a few poor scores. And if your business has been rating poorly in the past years, this gives you the chance to improve on your strategies on the platform.

Creating an Effective Facebook Marketing Campaign

Facebook's new rules can be daunting, especially if you haven't been using the platform as part of your wider online market strategy. The truth is that Facebook does not exactly demand that you follow a specific form of advertising to increase your brand's awareness there.

All it asks is that your campaign follows what it deems to be reflective on the needs and behavior of Facebook users. As such, when planning your marketing campaign on Facebook, there are several things that you have to keep in mind:

1. *Data is Important*

Any experienced advertiser knows that it is risky to venture into a new platform if you don't know the inner workings of that site. It is advisable, then, that you do your research first in identifying which markets have the highest possible chances in responding to any marketing you make, as this will save you a lot of time and money later on.

On Facebook, you have to always rely on the Insights tool, as it gives you a lot of data that will paint a picture as to how your target markets behave on the site. From when people engage with your content the most and the different demographic qualities that they share, the Insights tool can help you identify who you should target on the site and how to craft your message for them.

And the best part of the Insights tool is that it is free so you can do a lot of research without spending a single penny.

2. *Niche Down*

Generally speaking, mass appeal marketing has fallen out of favor in recent years as more laser-focused marketing styles are the norm. Fortunately for you, Facebook does offer some tools that allow you to improve on your ad's messaging so much so that a single ad can target different people differently despite carrying the same message.

For example, an owner of a Michelin-starred restaurant near a popular tourist spot in London might create two versions of the same advertisement. One might cater to people looking for a fine dining experience while another could cater to tourists and average food lovers.

In essence, the ad might say the same thing but it has been crafted in a way that it caters to three different mindsets. By identifying your niches and then molding your message according to those niches, you can ensure maximum engagement from your campaign without alienating one sector of your customer base.

3. *Stand Out Images*

In these times, a well-crafted message is no longer enough. That message has to be accompanied by something that can quickly catch the attention of your target audience.

This is where imagery comes into play, as a single image can be more compelling than one sprawling wall of text. That is regardless of how good a message that wall of text contains.

The good thing about imagery is that you are not exactly required to produce your own. All that is necessary is for the image to be relevant to the message that you are trying to convey. It also helps, however, if that image was legally acquired.

There are a number of sites out there that offer free stock photos for advertisers to use. You can also head to sites like Fiverr which helps you get in contact with image makers and photographers that can produce an image for your ad; for a reasonable price, of course.

And, with meme culture being quite thriving today (more on this later on), it is best that you take advantage of the fad and make your image meme-able. The more memorable it is, the more likely your advertisements will go viral on Facebook.

And we are all aware that going viral is synonymous with becoming famous on the Internet right now.

4. *Get Your Landing Page Right*

Always remember that any call to action you give in your message is only effective if you give your audience somewhere to follow through with their actions. A landing page allows your audience to learn more about your business while, at the same time, being exposed to more compelling offers.

Your landing page must be as well-designed as Facebook's current layout. This way, the experience that users have with your Facebook page remains the same when they click through your site. Also, it is at your site where most of your deals will be closed so make sure that navigating it is far from a frustrating experience.

5. *Focus on Sales, Not Clicks*

Engagement might be a strong signifier of an effective marketing campaign. However, it does not really assure your marketing campaign is helping people convert from audience members to paying customers.

There have been far too many instances when Facebook posts receive more than 100,000 comments, likes, and shares, but never translates to any action beneficial for you and your audience members. What good engagement is implying is that your ads are performing well. The question is if people are doing their part to enjoy the benefits you are claiming that your business offers on that ad.

What this only means is that you should never underestimate a good Call to Action. Create your CTAs so that they would actually prompt people to do something IMMEDIATELY after being exposed to your advertisements. On your part, you should also be diligent enough to track the sales of your business as soon as you publish your ads on Facebook.

Sales, after all, is the penultimate signifier that your marketing campaign on Facebook is truly effective.

You can craft all the compelling messages that you can think of. You can come up with the flashiest, meme-worthy ads on that platform.

But if none of those ads would result in people actually parting with their money to try out something that you have to offer, then you are wasting your time.

Facebook Live and How to Use It Effectively

The Live option on Facebook can make for a rather effective marketing tool if you know how to use it properly. It is one of way of keeping your content evergreen while also giving you the opportunity to interact with your target audience in real time while your live content is being aired.

So, is there a formula of success in using Facebook Live? Not really. How Live is used depends greatly on the message that you want to convey as well as the audience that you want to reach out to. However, there are a few things that you have to keep in mind to make the most out of this tool.

1. *The Introduction*

As odd as this might sound, you might want to greet your *replay* viewers first or, in some cases, only them. The reason for this is quite simple: Most live viewers don't exactly join you in the first few seconds after going live.

This also means that you should plan your script in as much as you would consider those who would re-watch your live feed in the future.

For your live viewers, you can easily greet them as they drop in. Facebook Live does offer you a tool where you can view the names of those that have just come into your feed. Keep your greetings short and mention your viewers by name (if you can, of course). Facebook users tend to connect with Live creators when they greet them by name in the middle of the broadcast.

2. *The Message*

This serves as the very core of your broadcast and should contain all bits of information that you want to talk about regarding a certain topic. First, you have to offer a brief description of what you are going to talk about. A few sentences should suffice in informing your audience about the nature of the discussion that is to follow.

For the sake of simplicity, divide your message into three or four main points. These sections allow your viewers to go through any sub-theme that they want on replay without having to go through the entire feed again.

Of course, this will help you once you are transcribing your live feed for use in other content that you will publish. By giving sub-topics to your discussion, you give your content creation team more topics to expound later on.

As for replying to comments, it is recommended that you get through your script first before you start engaging with your audience. Replying to comments can take up a lot of time and you run the risk of losing track of the topic you were trying to tackle.

3. *The End*

As you are about to end your live feed, try to wrap things up as neatly as possible. Give a summary of every topic that you have discussed, as this helps those who came in late to keep up with the rest of the group.

This is also where you can include your Call to Action. Suggest some actions that your viewers can do in response to the discussion that they have just taken part in. This might include subscribing to your page, buying your products/services, or heading to any other video or ad that you have on your page for more information.

If you are that particular with being consistent, you can also use this as an opportunity to announce when the next broadcast is going to air and encourage them to visit you on that date. With this, you give all your live feeds some form of coherence with one another, which keeps engagement high for all of your videos.

Preparing for a Live Broadcast

Facebook Live is a great tool for anyone who is used to being the center of attention. What happens, then, if you are not?

Being shy in your first ever Live feed is understandable. After all, you are entirely new to the experience and you might feel awkward with talking in front of a camera. Of course, there is still the need to keep the feed lively so your target audience does not disengage with you.

So, how can someone work through their stage fright and come out of a Live feed with their dignity intact? Here are a few tips to keep in mind.

1. ***Identify The Apprehension*** - What exactly is the reason why you are nervous in front of a camera? Is it because you are conscious with how you look, talk, and act? Are you afraid of the potential backlash you will suffer online?

The things that you are conscious about on a social level tends to answer why you are nervous with doing your Live feeds. Identify your fears first and your preparations would go smoothly from thereon.

2. ***Practice*** - This might sound cliché but practice does make perfect. Before hitting that Live button, make sure that you have gone through your script at least five times before. If you know what to say next, and are confident enough in saying it, you will fumble less once the feed starts.

Also, it would help if you can mentally condition yourself to the broadcast. Practicing gives you the chance to iron out any quirk you might have in delivering your lines as well as the expressions you subconsciously make when saying them.

3. ***Improvise*** - The one thing that you have to understand with live broadcasts is that even the best scripts can be ruined by unexpected happenings once the broadcast starts. Something might pop up in the middle of the broadcast, like your pet cat jumping onto your lap or you blurting out something stupid in the middle of your monologue.

This is where an ability to quickly recover from your mistakes would come in handy. You can actually learn a lot from actors and broadcasters who can take things in stride even if they are drifting off the script. As such, it is best that you watch online videos about news fails or improv comedy skits.

The point here is to reduce "dead space" in your broadcast while maintaining composure at all times. And speaking of dead space...

4. *Invest in a Teleprompter* - The one thing that can make any broadcast unnecessarily long is if you make constant pauses mid-sentence and use filler words like "um," "sort of," and "like." These fillers are usually uttered since your brain is trying to remember what to say next.

Practicing can remove a lot of these pauses and fillers but it would be better if you can invest in a teleprompter. This device can flash your script behind the camera to help you remember what to say next. And if a teleprompter is beyond your budget, you can always use the time-tested practice of having people flash "idiot boards" behind the camera during your broadcast.

Just remember that these tips will not ensure that your broadcast will go off without any problems. However, using these will help you deal with your own nervousness, which should make your broadcasts even more dynamic and lively.

Chapter 5: How to Market Your Business on Twitter

Twitter is home to 313 million active users every month, many of which belong to younger demographics. As such, generating enough of a following on this site depends greatly on how any business can adapt to the language and culture of the people using this platform.

Fortunately, starting a page on Twitter is a fairly straightforward affair. Once you fill out your bio, upload a picture, and come up with your Twitter handle, you can immediately start tweeting. However, what is not so simple is making your Twitter profile a potent marketing tool that generates leads and increases awareness of your brand.

So, how does one go about marketing their business on Twitter? There are many ways to do just that. But, before anything else, it's best to address a few issues first.

What Makes Twitter, well, Twitter?

Every social media platform out there requires a different approach and Twitter is no different. Basically, Twitter is a place where you are encouraged to share your thoughts within 140 characters or fewer.

As such, the platform focuses more on letting people engage with each other through active communication, not just publishing content for the consumption of the public. On sites like Facebook and YouTube, you are already good if you can constantly publish content at those sites through videos and status updates.

On Twitter, however, constantly tweeting is not enough. Your profile is expected to join in on conversations as they happen. It does this by replying to other tweets and sharing them. And you can expect for your own tweets to get commented and shared on, starting an entire conversation in itself.

Due to this, the primary name of the game on Twitter is *constant activity*. If you want to make your Twitter profile an effective marketing tool, you better have enough time in a day to make a status update on it.

And then there's the target markets you will find on the platform. And, like always, what you will be looking for here is constant activity.

So, in essence, you will not be looking for mere Twitter followers, but active ones as well. Where do you get these kinds of people? The answer is through Twitter Chats. These are moderated public discussions about a certain topic.

The Twitter Chats are filled with people who are constantly using their profiles to communicate with others in a certain sector of the platform. They are not just there to consume content but to do the one thing that Twitter wants its users to perform: Interact with other people.

As such, these are the kinds of people that you want to be exposed to your content as they are the ones that are going to reply, retweet, and share your content to their own circles.

There are Twitter chats for almost every topic and industry out there right now. If your business revolves around food service, you will definitely find more than a hundred Twitter chats dedicated to food. If your business sells toys and comic books, there are Twitter chats dedicated to all things found in Nerdom. And so on and so forth.

And what if you can't find a Twitter chat that fits your business? You start your own. This way, you carve out your own niche in Twitter's market which allows you to dictate the conversations that would occur there.

Marketing on Twitter the Right Way

So, you have a basic understanding of how Twitter is considerably different from other social media sites. So how do you go about marketing your business there? Keep in mind that what works for one business might not be so for another. Trial and error are to be expected in dealing with Twitter's ever-dynamic (and fickle) community.

But despite that, it's best that you learn what strategies other businesses have used to create awareness for their brand on the platform. Here are some of them:

1. *Planning Your Tweets Ahead*

Twitter's conversations are focused on the **Now** which is why it is recommended that you take a more active approach to your content planning for this platform. For example, if the Christmas season comes within a few weeks, you should already have planned the kind of content and tweets you are going to publish for that time of the year.

Planning ahead gives you the advantage of having enough time to craft your message while also coming up with hashtags that will most definitely trend for that season. For Christmas, we know that tags like #Christmas, #HappyHolidays, and #Mostwonderfultimeoftheyear will be definitely trending once December comes.

At best, you should have your campaigns ironed out three weeks ahead of the planned dates of their release. And once the big day comes, you can also follow up on other trending hashtags to go along with your more traditional marketing strategies.

The beauty with Twitter is that you can create content for events as they are happening instead of having to wait until they are over. This should keep hype and momentum for your campaigns at a high.

2. *Make It a Conversation*

A major gripe about business Twitter profiles is that their content is rather one-dimensional. What that means is that their tweets are simply broadcasts of whatever they want to send out to the community, not giving the community itself an opening where they can make that message into an active conversation.

This is not what Twitter is all about. Don't make your tweets just mere headlines with a link, a quote, or any brain fart that you can think of that day. Instead, give them a conversational tone.

There are several ways that you can do this which include the following:

A. **Make It a Question** - The reason for this is quite simple. Questions require answers which makes them perfect conversations starters.

B. **Reply** - If possible, allot 40% or 30% of your daily tweet responses to tweets made by other people. This helps you insert your business profile into ongoing conversations while also contributing to them. And speaking of contributing to a conversation...

C. **Add Your Own Insight** - If applicable, do not merely retweet somebody's content. Add your own insight into the statement regardless if you agree to it or not. Giving your own insight to tweets gives the impression that you have your own ideas and thoughts to share, like an actual human being that other people can interact with.

D. **Talk TO Your Audience** - Instead of the usual "Title of the Content-Link" format, try to make your links more of a conversation. You may start with a caption like "What do you think of this article?" before giving a link to that content.

The reason why you need to adopt a more conversational tone is that constant interaction increases your Twitter profile's activity. And the more active it is, the more visible it will be for Twitter's algorithms, which should increase your reach on the platform.

3. *Personalize*

Twitter folks love it when a business or a celebrity acknowledges their existence by responding to their tweets. As such, you should make the effort to respond to any tweet that tags you.

Granted, not a lot of these tweets require a response. Some are just looking for attention or finding an excuse to get refunded. Either way, people on Twitter need the assurance that you are listening to their complaints and opinions and are working on such issues to better improve your products/services.

Fortunately, Twitter gives you the option to craft a personalized response to customer queries and complaints. With this you can resolve any issue at a faster rate. This is also why Twitter is considered the best channel to air your customer complaints.

Granted, this does leave your business open to people who want to take advantage of your generosity. Look at the story of when a Twitter user tweets at Morton's steakhouse that he wants a porterhouse steak when he lands at the Newark Airport.

Sure enough, the user was greeted by a Morton's staff member with a plate of the porterhouse ready for consumption. This gave rise to a lot of copycats wanting their own personal slice of meat delivered to them at inopportune times. And so far, Morton's has yet to respond to succeeding requests, although the entire incident did generate enough good press for the business.

The lesson here is that you have to be careful with the tweets you are responding to and how you respond to them. The last thing that people expect is to have someone take their "joke" seriously, after all.

4. *Improving on Your Hashtag Game*

Hashtags are a core concept in Twitter's content sharing system as it can highlight certain hot topics and ongoing events, making your tweets relevant to the times.

And if somebody clicks on that hashtag, they will be linked to other tweets that talk about the same topic or subject. It's an easy way to embed yourself in an ongoing conversation while keeping your marketing up to date with the goings-on in your area.

However, it is also a fairly abused form of content and many business owners fail to use their hashtags effectively.

If you are planning to use hashtags in your Twitter marketing strategy, take the time to do it right. Keep the tags short and sweet, using only one or two words or short phrases.

For instance, if you are about to release some tweets that talk about preparing for winter, you can use words like #Winterready or, if you love pop culture references, a phrase like #Winteriscoming.

The point is to be creative and smart when using hashtags. The less boring your tags are, the more they will trend across the Twitter-verse.

5. *Use Visuals*

Twitter might be pushing for text-based content but that does not mean that images don't have a place on the site anymore. In fact, visuals are one way that you can spice up your tweets and keep their engagement at a high.

When making a tweet, find an image that would be relevant to the topic or is quirky enough to get everybody's attention. It doesn't even have to be an image that you produce on your own.

There are plenty of stock images on the Internet right now that you could get for free. Also, sites like Fiverr do feature professionals that can create an image for you for a fairly low price.

However, it is not necessary that every tweet comes with an image. A few image-centric tweets every five or ten texts, and link-based tweets, should be enough to break the monotony of your feed.

If done right, you should get thrice the engagement at most for your images compared to your other tweets.

6. *Use Humor*

Everybody loves a bit of levity here and there. As such, businesses that often inject humor in their tweets are most likely to get more retweets and comments than serious ones.

The reason for this is that humor is a language that almost everybody understands. Regardless of where a person comes from or what they believe in, they most definitely know what it takes to be funny.

There are a lot of Twitter profiles from businesses that use comedy to their favor. A chief example of this is the official Wendy's profile that started out tweeting mundane stuff but quickly adopted this personality of a sarcastic heckler when replying to tweets.

Another great example is Netflix, whose tweets contain a lot of inside jokes and references of their popular shows. And who could forget about Spirit airlines poking fun at themselves for any mishap that their flights encounter?

Warning: In as much as effective comedy is in improving engagement for your tweets, you must know the right kind of humor to use. There are certain jokes or phrases that could be misconstrued as offensive to a lot of people.

If possible, don't make light of subjects like race, religion, mental illness, gender identities, and physical disabilities. The best kind of clean humor today are cultural references and snarky comebacks, so use those if you have to be funny.

Also, it is best that you do not make light of a recent tragedy. Dark humor is not for everyone and those that do get offended by your quips will respond negatively. And there are no shortages of examples for people and businesses that got their Twitters shut down due to a tone-deaf tweet.

7. *Peak Hour Tweeting*

Depending on the time zone, there are hours in a day when users are the most active. This is where people are going to be the most likely to interact with your content.

As such, you have to know when your audience is going to be at their most active on Twitter. This way, you can time your tweets with their peak activity which boosts engagement and click-through rates for your content.

Research has shown that Friday going into the weekend is where people are at their most active compared with Monday to Thursday. Also, the times where people are at their most active span from 12PM to 6PM during the weekends and then 12PM to 3PM during the work days.

However, your peak posting time will also be dependent on the behavior of your target audience. If you are targeting teenagers, you can expect for their tweet hours to be more sporadic. Normally, teenagers are the most active before school starts, during lunch, and then after the final period of that day.

For adults, however, the 12PM-6PM range is more consistent due to work.

You can automate the scheduling of your posts through apps like Hootsuite and Buffer. These programs allow you to input a certain time and date where a tweet will automatically go live. This way, you can go about marketing your business without having to remember when and where you are going to publish a tweet.

8. *Use Twitter Video*

If images get a lot of attention, then videos get even more than what images could generate. Twitter right now has a function where profiles can upload an existing video footage or capture one live for the rest of the world to follow.

Studies have shown that videos are most likely to be retweeted six to ten times more than images and text. The reason for this is that videos have a multimedia appeal to them and have generally longer lifespans compared to other content as far as relevance is concerned.

Also, you could get to show more to your audience through a video than you would through text and images. With videos, you may give your audience a behind the scenes look at your business or allow them to know the people running your business more intimately.

If you are seriously considering producing video content, you might want to invest on proper recording equipment. A good camera and a microphone is a must if you want people to interact with your videos more. However, a decent camera phone would do the trick especially if you find yourself in the middle of an event that needs to be shared to Twitter.

9. *Optimizing Your Bio*

Although your Bio can only contain 160 characters, it can say much about your business's personality as well as its goals. As such, you need to create a bio that will catch anyone's attention, and this is a rather straightforward process.

When creating your bio, always think of that 160-character box as an opportunity to say to the world why this business exists and the goals you want to accomplish through it.

When creating your Twitter bio, there are a few tips that you need to keep in mind.

A. **Be Accurate** - Tell the people what your brand is about and what your business offers.

B. **Use Creativity** - Always inject a bit of creativity and humanity in your bio. Crack a joke, say something profound, or tell people what you love the most. The more relatable your bio is, the more engagement your page is going to experience.

C. **Brag** - It doesn't hurt to tell people what you have accomplished so as long as they are real. If you've been in the industry for quite a while, let the people know. If you've won some awards, let the people know.

D. **Target** - Write your bio so that it fits the language and the needs of your target audience. If your business targets teens, you can use an informal tone. And if you are targeting an older audience, a bit of formality wouldn't hurt either.

E. **Hashtag It -** This will link your bio to topics and events that your business usually covers.

10. *Do an Advanced Search*

Have you always wondered what people feel about your business or the kind of products/services that it offers? You can do this through Twitter's Advanced Search feature.

If you are not in the middle of tweeting or replying to somebody's tweet, take the time to feel how your industry is faring through Twitter's search engine.

For instance, if you run a clothing store, you can type terms like "clothes" or "fashion" or even "apparel" into the search bar. You will most likely find a person looking for someone that can provide them with those or what people in general think about businesses like yours.

This is a good way of determining whether or not your business has a sizeable audience on Twitter. And the tweet you discovered can be an opportunity for you to convert that user into a paying customer. As such, take the time to reply and answer their query.

11. *Start a Poll*

Polls are one of the most actionable forms of content in any social media platform right now. Fortunately, creating a poll is not hard as you only need to click on the Poll option when creating your tweet, and then add the options and the question.

Twitter polls have a double function if it is not apparent to you. First, they can boost engagement to your page, as the poll requires people to perform specific actions. This way, you can initiate a multi-layered conversation with your audience with just one tweet.

However, polls can also act as market research where you can get an idea as to which products people or service people consume the most as well as their purchasing decisions. With this, you can mold your future marketing campaigns to better resonate with your audience and even improve on your actual business offerings.

12. *End with a Compelling Call to Action*

Always remember that the point of your Twitter marketing campaign is to help generate leads and improve on your click-through rates. As such, if your marketing does not prompt people to do any action that would benefit them and you, your effort is pointless no matter how well-done it was.

Your Call to Action must contain a clear and concise statement as to what you want your audience to do after hearing the message. Whether it is subscribing to you or heading to your main website, the CTA must contain a request that people can perform easily.

When crafting your CTA, you might want to look into a few action phrases such as:

- Please follow us
- Visit our site
- Click here
- Download this file
- Go to our sales page
- Visit us at (insert your business address or website here)
- Learn more
- Don't forget to click like/retweet/share

An effective CTA is bound to drive engagement to your page which should funnel traffic to your main website. And if that CTA is then validated by equally good products and services, those coming from your Twitter page might just convert into paying customers.

What Does it Mean to Get Verified?

The process of receiving that blue badge at the end of your profile can be convoluted and demanding. And there are successful Twitter handles that have millions of followers and can funnel a large volume of traffic to their website without being verified by Twitter itself.

So, this does beg the question: should you want to be verified by Twitter? That is up to you.

But if you do want to become verified on the platform, you must know what you are getting yourself into.

A. <u>Advantages</u>

A key advantage in becoming verified is the assurance of an increase in followers. That blue badge/check mark on your profile does count as social proof as it implies that Twitter itself has checked your profile and found it to be legit and meeting their community standards.

And that social proof does make things easier on your part as a marketer. Since Twitter trusts your profile, people are going to become more responsive to your content. Also, content coming from verified users do experience a spike in engagement as their tweets get responded to, shared, and retweeted the most.

Also, verification does substantially change the layout of your profile. You might notice that there is now a separate column for mentions and follower notifications as well as a column for follows coming from other verified profile.

This way, you can easily identify the kind of engagement your pages are getting which should help you in improving your marketing campaign.

B. Disadvantages

As Uncle Ben would say: "With great power comes great responsibility." Becoming verified on Twitter, as such, comes with a number of responsibilities that you are expected to uphold.

One of these responsibilities is in making sure that your bio contains factual information. There have been far too many instances of verified Twitter handles losing their status, as their bios are not accurately reflecting what that person is doing. You could not even change it frequently or you would risk losing your verified status.

Also, Twitter now is going to closely monitor your profile. Any infraction that would have otherwise been looked over in the past would now heavily affect your profile. As such, becoming familiar with Twitter's ever-expanding Community Guidelines is something that all verified handles are expected to do.

Another major drawback with the verified status is the sense of dilution it currently experiences. There are too many verified handles right now so the value of becoming verified is not as highly regarded as it was in the past.

Lastly, the increase of visibility comes with an increase to one's exposure to negative elements. Attacks on verified handles are far too frequent in recent years. In fact, Twitter recommends that you use a two-step verification process to protect your profile from the Internet's more insidious elements.

The Verification Process

Twitter has never exactly laid out how they verify profiles on their platform. They do not even give a specific timetable as to when accounts might get verified.

However, what is known is that the process of becoming verified involves several steps. This includes:

- Scanning and e-mailing a copy of documents that would confirm your identity and that of your business.

- Listing out a set of reasons why you are worthy of attaining a verified status.

- Links of outside sources that mention or confirm the existence of your person and that of your business.

Depending on how strong a case you present, becoming verified can take between two weeks to several years. This is because Twitter also has to double-check your background while also looking for duplicate accounts on their site.

So, in essence, becoming verified can really help in your marketing efforts. However, reaching that status also implies that you have to do more to appease Twitter's community standards while shielding yourself from negative online entities.

If you are willing to shoulder the risks it entails, then following the verification process might be a worthwhile effort.

Chapter 6: Dominating in YouTube

Being the second largest social media site in the world, you could definitely see how potent of a marketing platform YouTube can be. And if you are one that would like to get famous, let us just say that YouTube is the Internet's counterpart to Hollywood.

If set up right, your YouTube page can drive a lot of traffic to your websites which should improve your rankings on Google's SERPs.

Here's the thing, though. YouTube, in recent years, is not exactly known for being consistent or lenient. If you want to really make full use of the platform, you will have to play by YouTube's rules—whatever form those rules take.

So What Works in YouTube Now?

YouTube is quite malleable as a platform since it is always changing the rules of what is acceptable there. Since you are going to be improving on your presence there NOW, it is best that you know what would work on YouTube in the current year. This includes:

1. *Focus on Watch Time*

YouTube's algorithm used to rank videos by the number of click-throughs they received. The more clicks a video gets, the better its rank will be.

This, of course, led to an abuse of the system when users started posting clickbait to lure viewers in. This was quite the rage in 2014 when videos were titled with something ridiculous like "OMG! You Won't Believe What Happens Next!" only for the content to show nothing that is unbelievable or out of the ordinary.

As a countermeasure, YouTube changed the algorithm by making it focus more on how long people stay in the video as opposed to how many times that video got clicked through.

For example, a 20-minute video would not rank well if people drop out of the page by the 5 or 10 minute mark. But a 5-minute video where people actually managed to reach the end of would receive better rankings on the search page.

For this reason, it can be seen why YouTube's recommended page is filled with movie trailers, music videos, talk show segments, and other shorter content that is easier to digest.

2. *Production Value is Rarely Important*

Don't get the wrong idea. It is still necessary that your video should be easy to go through. The video quality must be good and the audio loud enough to be picked up on any device.

It is just that interaction and consumption matter more these days than good production values. One big proof of this is the surge of podcasts and commentary channels on the page where every video is comprised of nothing more than one or a handful of people talking in front of a camera.

And then there are channels like the now-defunct FilthyFrankTV. Despite featuring videos shot in a dorm room and featuring people wearing cheap spandex onesies, Filthy Frank's videos get quite a lot of engagement even as of 2019.

The point is that people now don't care how much you spend in creating your videos. If the message you are trying to convey resonates with them a lot, your rankings should be decent in the search page.

3. *More Subscriptions*

As of now, visibility can also be affected by a channel's subscription count. How this works is actually quite simple: When a person subscribes to a channel, all of the videos that that channel has published will sporadically show up on their feed. And if that channel produces new content, its subscribers will get a notification of such.

In essence, YouTube is personalizing each user's feed by subtly feeding that user content that they think that person would like. If you, for example, would subscribe to a review channel like the Nostalgia Critic, you will also get recommendations for other similar channels like Red Letter Media, Jeremy Jahns, and Chris Stuckmann.

On your part, this means that you should really consider improving the content of your Call to Action. Reminding viewers to like, subscribe, and turn the notification button on is one way of making sure that the reach of your channel is optimized.

How to Get Better Rankings in YouTube

This might come as a surprise to you but the rules that apply in the Search Engine Optimization process also apply in YouTube's rankings. In essence, the ranking you will get there is going to be dependent on your content's presentation, relevance, and, to some extent, quality. To boost your content's rankings, there are a few tips that you have to keep in mind.

1. *The Title*

The first thing that a search engine bot in YouTube goes through when looking for content that answers a query is the title. As a rule of thumb, you have to make your title attractive enough but would reflect the content of the video. If, for example, you are about to publish a video about the top ten street foods in your local area, then the title should contain the words "street foods," "top 10," and whatever the name of your local area is.

Also, only be clever with your titling if it is really necessary. Save the sarcasm for the actual video because search engine bots are artificial intelligence and artificial intelligence still can't understand humor. Or nuance. Their purpose is to check if your title has the right keywords that would match the query being asked.

2. *Add Closed Captions*

People absorb information in different ways. Some are content with just video or audio but a lot of people cannot get a full experience of your content unless they also have something to read. Of course, there is the fact that some people are just hard of hearing or have bad sound systems.

This is where closed captioning comes into play, and it is best that you add them on the video itself or through YouTube's closed captioning feature at the options once the video is published.

With YouTube's closed captioning feature, you can add subtitles yourself or allow strangers to do it for you.

YouTube also has auto-generated subtitles, but they are a work in progress. They can't properly translate what you are saying, especially if you have an accent or speak too fast.

If possible, let another human being write your video's transcript so the message does not get lost in translation.

3. *Descriptions Matter*

The descriptions section in your video can help a person get the gist of the message without actually watching the video. This way, they can decide whether or not to continue watching your content.

When adding the descriptions of your video, always follow the rule of KISS: Keep it Short and Simple.

The reason for this is that YouTube tends to cut descriptions that are longer than 150 characters and hide the rest through the "Show More" option. This gives viewers another option whether to read the description or not. Most of them would choose the latter.

Also, it is at your discretion where you can direct your audience to your other web pages through a CTA. As such, make sure to link all the relevant pages of your site for your video there.

4. *Thumbnails Matter*

In 2018, YouTube ran an experiment where an automated program would decide on the thumbnail for a video using stills of the footage. Let us just say that it was not warmly received.

If possible, always create the thumbnail yourself. You can choose a certain section of the video, edit it, add enhancements, and then add your title. You can also use a separate image provided that you paid for it or ask permission from the image's owner.

Whatever the case, make sure that the image is of good quality and would also reflect the content of the video

.

5. *Every Minute Counts*

Many people think that YouTube is biased towards longer videos. The truth is that the algorithm now values videos that offer a lot of content per minute.

For example, if your video only has five minutes of actual content, then the footage you upload should have the same length. With this, viewers can find your content to be valuable, encouraging them to finish it. And if the stay time for your videos is high, they will rank better at YouTube's search page.

One thing you should never do is to add "blank space" in between or at the end of your videos to pad your content. Prior to the algorithm change, a channel by the name of LeafyisHere was notorious for adding minute-long blank spaces in their video to make it look like they have 10 minutes of content. Needless to say, engagement for the channel dropped severely when the new algorithm was put in place.

The Adpocalypse: How to Survive It

Aside from being a marketing tool, your YouTube channel can help you earn a bit of money through every advertisement being shown in the middle of your videos. However, YouTube insists that your content must be "ad friendly" if you want to monetize on it.

As of 2019, YouTube has experienced three Adpocalypses, events wherein all channels suffered from severe loss of monetization when their videos did not meet YouTube's current standards. Since an Adpocalypse acts like YouTube's very own state of calamity, you need to survive these events. Here's how:

1. *Always Check on the Community Guidelines*

More often than not, an Adpocalypse is triggered whenever YouTube makes a change in their algorithm following changes in their community guidelines. The actual guideline is quite extensive but the point is that your video should be seen as friendly for advertisers in order to be monetized.

And what is ad friendly in YouTube now? This could mean a lot of things including not showing explicit content, not promoting violence, and is respective of current sensitive social issues. Also, keeping the language clean can help keep your videos monetized.

In early 2018, YouTube star Logan Paul was hit hard by one Adpocalypse after a series of videos involving playing with dead animals and showing a victim in Japan's infamous suicide forest. Other smaller channels were also hit the hardest for a single curse word, showing inappropriate items, and other things that YouTube finds offensive.

2. *Beware of Fair Use*

Using somebody's content without permission is another way of getting demonetized. When you use even a piece of footage or music owned by another channel/company, you will be hit with a copyright strike. If your channel gets struck out, you will find that you can't monetize on your video until the dispute is resolved. Worse, you may not even be able to upload content for weeks on end.

If possible, credit the people that own the music or footage that you are going to use for your videos, especially if such content lasts longer than five seconds. Another option is to use Royalty-free music such as the ones created by Internet artist Kevin Macleod. This should prevent your channel from getting a copyright strike or, at the very least, a legit one.

3. *Find Other Ways of Monetization*

Instead of relying on YouTube's ad revenue, some creators on the site have turned to places like Patreon for earnings. This way, they can directly interact with their audience and ensure that they have enough to stay afloat for the next few months.

Of course, since you already have a business, you can always use your videos to market your products and services. You can even use your offerings as the core subject for your videos. You may even teach people tricks on how to deal with certain problems, giving central focus to what your business offers.

If done right, the content you post on YouTube should help funnel traffic to your main web pages which should keep revenues coming from your online front at a high. And if your content matches what YouTube deems acceptable, you can even earn a bit of money on the side from advertisements.

What Content Should You Produce?

Of course, you are expected to publish videos on YouTube. The question is what kind of videos should you create for the site?

There is exactly no straightforward answer to this, as anything technically goes on YouTube. However, for marketing campaigns, your videos should find a balance between two different needs: the audience and your brand.

The Brand

What makes your brand stand out from the rest of the competition? What does it stand for? How do you make it competitive?

You could answer this by going to your business's vision and mission statement, which should also tell you of your brand's identity. What you should come up with, then, is a list of qualities that can give your content marketing plan a direction of sorts to follow.

Aside from your business's inner qualities, you should also find out what makes your brand ownable. What makes it resonate with the target market? What makes it appealing to people?

The Audience

Obviously, this is your target audience and finding them on YouTube is easy. Basically, they are more or less the same kinds of people that will form your primary target market. For example, if your brand is catered towards young adults, then your YouTube audience will be comprised of young adults.

By finding out who your audience is, you have an idea as to why they would visit your YouTube channel in the first place. And for this, you need to establish their intent.

For instance, if your business delves into carpentry and DIY home remodeling projects, your YouTube audience will come to your videos with the intent to learn new carpentry skills or how to complete certain DIY projects.

But intent is not always measured by tangible products and services. More often than not, your YouTube audience is there to feel good about themselves. Self-gratification is a major reason why people subscribe to channels. In fact, channels like Pewdiepie, h3h3, and Markiplier gain success by making people laugh and feel good about themselves.

The point is if you know what makes your audience tick, you should have no problems in determining what kind of content you should produce on your channel. Once this is done, all that is left to do is to plan on how you go about creating content for the channel.

Feeding the Demand

There is actually no way that you can satisfy the demand from your market with just one video. The trick with YouTube is to gradually build engagement with your brand through a growing library of content with different themes, messages, and even formats.

This may be a daunting task to look at but it is actually easy to pull off and manage. All you have to remember is three C's:

Create, Collaborate, and Curate.

1. Create

This covers the content that you create for your channel. Your content should give the impression that it was made by people who understood the brand and would represent the brand.

Content can be made to perform various roles. It can invoke emotions, it can inform and educate, it can teach new skills, and it can entertain.

At this point, the goal is to be consistent with your goals for your YouTube channel and with your overall marketing campaign.

Large companies often use this scheme with their YouTube marketing campaigns by making their videos share the same message despite having different themes and formats.

Also, movie studios do this in promoting their big budget films. When a movie nears its release date, you might find that your feed will be bombarded with trailers, teasers, and clips promoting the same film.

2. *Collaborate*

If you have the resources and the clout, you can start doing collaborations with other content creators and promote both brands in tandem. The goal at this phase is to extend the reach and influence of your channel in YouTube's community of content creators.

One fine example of this is the Fine Brothers, who constantly invite celebrities to react to recent trends and memes. Even companies like Pepsi team up with smaller channels to create videos that entertain people while pushing up certain products.

3. *Curate*

Once you have built a library of videos on your channel, what are you going to do with them all? In most cases, small channels would have these videos removed but you can always use your audience to help you curate your videos.

For example, you publish a video that contains updates on a developing story. You can say in your CTA to head on to other videos where you covered the previous parts of the story (with links, of course). This is what is called curating and it is a good way to funnel traffic through each of your videos, which boosts the visibility of your channel.

Another thing that you can do is to give your viewers a chance to dictate what happens next in an ongoing story. For example, if a video gets X amount of comments, you might release another video following one story path but if it reaches X amount of likes, you follow a second story path.

Curation is a good way to keep your audiences engaged, especially if they know that they have a say in how your content flows. It's also one way to keep your old content evergreen while producing new ones constantly.

Clickbait and How to Avoid It

Clickbait is any form of content that does not reflect the one promised in the title. As far as YouTube is concerned, clickbaiting your audience is one underhanded way of increasing engagement for your channel and they don't tolerate it.

Why YouTube hates clickbait is quite obvious. YouTube has always been pushing to regulate the revenue streams on its platform and would encourage creators to grow their viewer base in the most natural way possible.

Basically, every click on that video is a potential source of revenue. Understanding this, a lot of content creators abused the system by creating undeserved interest for their videos.

Since YouTube is insistent that you grow your channel naturally, you must follow their community guidelines in titling and describing your videos. And to do that, there are a few tips that you have to keep in mind.

1. *Honesty Is Always the Best Policy*

Clickbait, by design, aims to mislead viewers. The problem became so prevalent in the mid-2010s that YouTube started a crackdown on clickbait, causing a lot of channels to drop in their rankings.

When creating your title, always follow the age-old policy in journalism: Keep things neutral and informative. If your video is about the seven ways that you can use floor polish, then the title should reflect that. If it is about the reasons why you should visit the Eiffel Tower, then the title should say so.

Nothing added, nothing taken.

2. *Ease Up on the Hyperbole*

Hyperbole and advertising used to go hand in hand but the overuse of exaggeration has hurt more brands in recent years. Words like "The Best" or "Greatest" are okay since they are still open to interpretation.

What is not okay, however, is if you start getting ridiculous with your title's wording. Phrases like "OMG!" or "Your Jaw Will Drop with..." or even "Number 10 Will Cause You to Faint" just reek of desperation on your part. It is as if you don't have enough faith in your viewers to find your content valuable as is.

The solution? Let your video do the talking. Make the title in such a way that it merely gives viewers an impression of what to expect if they click through the video's link.

97

3. *Drop the Exclamation Points*

Bangorreah is an annoying trend in storytelling where the creator relies too much on exclamation points just to get their point across or make things more dramatic than they really are.

Several years ago, you might have noticed videos with annoying titles like "Don't Try This at Home!!!!!!" or "What was He Thinking? Lolololol!!!!!" It's an eyesore at best and is a telltale sign of amateurish writing on the creator's part.

If possible, limit your punctuation to commas and semicolons. They can give viewers hints as to what to expect from the video without making the title needlessly long or dramatic.

And, as for the question mark, use this only if your content does encourage people to engage in a conversation. Also, Google loves question-type content recently as it matches the usual queries made in the search engine now.

To summarize, make sure that your videos are titled to encourage people to click through. But never, in any case, dupe your viewers into thinking that they will receive something when you have clearly another thing prepared for them.

In Summary

Out of all the social media sites out there, YouTube can look like the most unpredictable. What worked just barely a year ago would no longer apply with the platform's penchant for constant algorithm updates.

What you have to understand is that YouTube has its own interests to protect. With advertisers using the platform for their marketing, they would want to make sure that the content that they produce reflects things that the general public would find to be marketable and inoffensive.

What this means for you is to constantly toe the line if you want your channel to become an effective marketing tool for your business. Keep your content clean and ad friendly and you should not receive any serious strike. And, fortunately for you, you can make your channel visible on YouTube without having to betray the qualities that make your brand unique.

Chapter 7: Instagram and the Age of the Influencer

Out of all the social media sites out there, it seems that Instagram is the one that is the oddest. There is nothing about it that screams "great for marketing businesses" at first glance.

However, Instagram can make for a rather effective marketing tool if you know how to use it properly. But, before anything else, you have to understand why Instagram can make for a valid platform to market your business on. Here are a few facts:

1. It is the third largest social media platform with over 800 million active users every day. 80% of the population is made up of private individuals while the rest are taken up by businesses, large corporations, and other legal entities.

2. The biggest market segment here comes from people ages 18 to 30. this means that Instagram is frequented by teenagers and adults who are quite known for their active spending habits.

3. Approximately 51% of all known active users log in to their accounts on Instagram at least once every day.

4. Instagram stories have been used by nearly 37.5% of the user base and a third of these stories are generated by business profiles.

5. A highly visual platform, 58% of all recorded engagements on Instagram come from photos.

6. The most used hashtags on the platform are #fashion, #Instagood, and #love.

7. Engagement peaks at the platform during 4pm to 5am, regardless of the time zone.

8. There is no popular filter used in the platform, as the best engaged photos do not have one.

9. On a monthly basis, Instagram is visited by two million active users. As such, the potential for advertising is particularly strong on the platform.

10. A typical Instagram profile can net as much as 600 followers and can follow approximately 350 accounts. And this is even if the account is rarely visited on a daily basis.

So What Makes Instagram a Valid Marketing Tool?

On a more technical standpoint, what does make Instagram great for marketing? The answer will be different from one business owner to another. But, on general terms, there are three features that make the platform stand out from other social media sites.

1. *It's Mobile-Friendly by Default*

Since mobile users already take up a third of the population of Internet users today, it goes without saying that a website that is optimized for navigation through mobile devices is going to thrive. Instagram is not optimized for mobile devices per se. It was designed from the ground up to accommodate mobile users.

In essence, Instagram allows you to create your profile and start sharing content using only a few tools and, better yet, requires you to rely on only two fingers. If you set up your profile right, you can expose yourself to a near-infinite scroll of new content every time you are logged in to the platform.

2. *A Visual Medium*

It is kind of a standard now in marketing to use visuals due to their potential to generate a lot of engagements. Fortunately, Instagram's design encourages you to use visual content for your marketing. In fact, the best engaged content on the platform can be comprised of mostly images and with minimal alterations at that.

As for image sizing, Instagram automatically converts all images to the same size. This way, your images are not disproportionately too large or too small, giving your Instagram campaigns a sense of uniformity.

3. *Strong Staying Power*

What makes Instagram instantly distinct from other platforms is the sheer simplicity of using it. It has an interface that is easy to understand and most of its features are available with just a few clicks on different pages.

This makes the platform easy for younger demographics to express themselves and for businesses to do their marketing without having to master its technical aspects. It also helps that Instagram's online community has a vibe and a sense of togetherness that no other social media platform has managed to replicate...yet.

But not everything is well and good with Instagram. As with other social media platforms, Instagram has some quirks that users have to contend with. Here are a few of them:

1. *No Links*

You can't just include links in your posts at Instagram unless you find a way to embed them into your images. Alternatively, you can have your links placed on your profile but this means that you have to regularly change them if you want your audience to be directed to a specific page relevant to the campaign you are implementing.

The reason why Instagram does this is to prevent users from spamming links on their posts. If you want your campaigns to funnel traffic to your site from this platform, you will have to get creative.

2. *Text is Almost Worthless*

As a highly visual medium, any campaign that relies a lot on text will not be effective here. You have to understand that people come to Instagram for images that they can share to other people which means that you have to master how to deliver your message here using only a few words.

At best, incorporate your text as part of your images and keep them short. To say it differently, let your images do the marketing for you.

3. *No Dialogue*

Unlike other social media platforms, Instagram does not exactly encourage people to engage with each other in a conversation. The platform just wasn't designed for it.

If conversations lie at the heart of your marketing campaign, it is best that you find a way to change how your messages are being conveyed if you want to succeed on the platform.

How to do Marketing on Instagram

Despite its disadvantages, making your handle on Instagram stand out from the competition is not exactly complicated. Regardless of the marketing campaign you will come up with, there are some tips that you could follow to increase the reach of your profile and better engage with your target audience. Here are some of them:

1. *Get a Business Profile*

When setting up your Instagram handle, make sure that it is set up for businesses. Aside from helping people identify that your handle is for a legitimate commercial entity, a business profile has a few added benefits that are exclusive to this profile type.

- **The Contact Button** - This allows your followers to quickly contact you through the platform.

- **Insights** - Instagram gives business profile handlers the ability to gauge the engagement of their content as soon as it is published.

- **Advertising Tools** - Instagram gives businesses some tools to create advertisements and monitor them throughout the entire campaign. And the best part with these tools is that they are not as difficult to master as the ones currently found on Facebook.

- **Instant Exposure** - As a business profile, your handle has better chances of having its content seen in the feeds of your target audience.

2. Collaborate with an Influencer

An influencer can act as middleman between you and younger demographics and there are quite a lot of them on Instagram. So, the question: Which influencer is the right kind for your business?

To answer that question, you will first have to determine if both you and the influencer share the same target markets. It does not have to be a 100% match, mind you. You only have to make sure that you and that person have been reaching out to roughly the same kinds of people in your advertising campaigns.

Then, you will have to check if their overall style of communicating with people matches yours. You can see this from the way they express themselves and generate attention based on the topics that they usually handle.

Lastly, you have to make sure that their overall demeanor and language matches your image. If, for example, you have fashioned an image for your business as a professional establishment, you don't hire an influencer that goes out of their way to stir controversy. Of course, such styles would work for certain businesses but not for all.

3. *Cross Promote*

One way to easily increase traffic from your Instagram to your other web pages is to promote the fact that you can also be found elsewhere. Think of it this way: Most of your Instagram followers also have profiles on Facebook and Twitter and tend to frequent YouTube for videos. Also, they are quite active in surfing through the Internet.

So why not encourage them to look for you in other markets that you happen to be operating in too?

With cross promotions, you can increase the exposure for each of the content you publish on Instagram while also consolidating the traffic for all of your advertising channels and main web pages. If done right, you can even cut down on costs for creating new content, as you don't have to create content specifically for one site only.

Why Consider Using Influencers in Your Campaign?

The word "influencer" is casually thrown around these days but that does not mean that their overall impact on your marketing campaigns has diminished. In fact, your marketing campaign on Instagram (or in social media in general) can even be more successful if you are backed by a few influencers here and there.

So, this does give rise to the question: Why should you even consider letting these people into your marketing? Here are a few reasons.

1. *Millennials Don't Trust Big Business*

It might be because they were born at the dawn of the Internet Age that millennials are a rather cynical bunch. Millennials tend to look at advertising with a certain sense of disdain and are not too keen when businesses invade the social media sites that they frequent.

This means that you and other businesses will have to face the challenge of connecting with these people in a way that is not forced. And not only do you have to establish a connection with them, you will also have to find a way to make them convert into paying customers.

So, if advertisers and businesses are not as trusted as they were in the past, who do millennials trust? To put it simply, they tend to trust the people that they see the most online and can interact with their audience in a personal and direct manner. And that is where influencers have the advantage over you.

2. *Traditional Advertising is No Longer Effective*

If millennials are typically wary of businesses and advertising these days, it also means that the conventional ways of advertising products and services to them are not going to work. One good example of this is the fact that younger people don't watch as much TV today compared to older generations.

It's not that they can't access cable TV as older folks do. It is just that they tend to find the information that they need through the Internet.

And even conventional online marketing strategies have failed to generate considerable engagement from this demographic. Most people at the age of 18 and 30 now know what AdBlock is and have activated it for their browsers. This means that the chances that paid marketing content is going to show up whenever they browse through the Internet or watch a YouTube video is drastically lowered.

On the other hand, influencers can get younger people to listen to them. Whether it is because these influencers are millennials themselves or just know how to connect with younger people, there is the fact that younger demographics are more receptive to them today than your trusted advertising strategies.

3. Clout

When you collaborate with an influencer, you will notice that they can easily convince younger people to do what they want. The reason for this is simple: Influencers tend to bring a sense of humanity in social media which traditional advertisers lack. Of course, people tend to trust humans more than they do brands.

So, if an influencer can convince their audience to trust your brand, then younger folks will have no qualms about establishing a relationship with your business.

Of course, how strong that relationship is will be dependent on the influencer. But it cannot be denied that they enjoy a unique kind of trust that is placed on them by their very own audience.

Of course, even with all these reasons, there are some instances when an influencer is not necessary. There are even talks about the trend dropping recently due to some influencers abusing the trust that people have placed on them.

Despite that, it would be best that you give your brand a human connection. And in a platform that is dependent on visuals, having that human connection is vital to the survival of your brand there.

To Conclude

There is no denying that Instagram has its own set of quirks that you have to deal with. However, that does not mean that its viability as a serious marketing platform is diminished.

What is required from you is to understand the basic design of the website while also adapting to the unique culture its community has established for the platform. And if you do provide the kind of content that Instagram people consume the most, the rest, as they say and with no pun intended, will follow.

Chapter 8: PR in the World of Social Media

Believe it or not, a good public relations strategy goes hand in hand with any marketing push. However, not a lot of businesses can get it right.

It is either that they don't generate enough interest for their stories or have not properly established the channels necessary to get their PR across.

On the other hand, good PR can enhance any marketing campaign for even a fraction of the budget. This is made possible, of course, if you know the basis of it.

What Makes PR So Effective?

The first thing that you would wonder is why bother with PR in the first place? After all, it is not the only tool out there that you can use to generate enough of a buzz around your social media channels.

If there is one thing that PR brings that could be summed up in on word, it would be *credibility*.

How this works is actually quite clever. Any marketing campaign that you create is simply just that, an advertisement. This means that people can still tune you out, especially if the image you are projecting in your campaigns does not reflect your brand in real life.

However, if you put that same message in the context of something uplifting like, say, a news report, people will tend to be more receptive

The reason for this is that the mere mention of a product or service in a passive tone in a narrative tends to act as a subtle form of endorsement. In fact, CTAs are more effective when done with PR as opposed to pure marketing content.

Public Relations and the Search Engine Optimization Process

The thing about PR and the SEO process is that you can synergize your efforts in both fields to come up with quite interesting results. A good PR-SEO strategy could yield you a number of benefits which include the following.

1. *Linking*

Linking remains a particularly important factor in search engine algorithms. The problem, however, is that getting good links is becoming difficult in recent years.

With PR, you can have your content linked to some influential websites, which can funnel quite a lot of traffic to your social media channels and web pages. For instance, a mere mention of your content at sites like Huffington Post can get your brand exposed to even more people, resulting in a significant boost in your web traffic.

2. <u>Better Brand Recognition</u>

The search engine bots scour information in a way that is seemingly similar to how we humans do it. Basically, they will look for any mention of your brand name through either your primary channels or through third-party sources. The more your brand gets mentioned, the more visible it will be in the SERPs.

It won't even matter if your business is small compared to larger, well-established companies. If your business gets mentioned in the same breath as the industry's most influential people, your pages should at least rank decently in the results pages.

3. <u>Improving on Your Reputation</u>

How do people typically encounter a new business or brand? If you answer "reviews," then you are correct. For instance, the reputation of restaurants and their ability to get more people in is utterly dependent nowadays on what people say about them on websites like Yelp.

Chances are that people would even trust whatever those reviews say more than what you say about yourself in your marketing campaigns.

The obvious problem here, of course, is that people can be notoriously fickle. There have been far too many instances in the past where businesses have been "review bombed" on third-party websites just because the owner said something that they didn't like.

This would naturally lead to rankings for that business dropping in the SERPs.

However, this is where a PR strategy would come into play, as it can alleviate most of that negative impact brought about by poor reviews. With enough mentions of your web pages, your ranking should remain at the first SERP.

In essence, good PR helps you gain a bit of control over your reputation in the online community, even if a lot of people still don't like you.

4. *Social Proof*

So what is your normal reaction if some big business or third-party website mentions your brand? Of course, you are going to brag about that.

What you have to remember is that big sites like Huffington Post, New York Times, or other publications with handles on social media are considered reliable sources of information. As such, a mention of your business makes your business even more trustworthy.

In other words, people will hesitate less in engaging with your business if it has appeared in stories published in major publications.

Of course, that story has to show you in a positive light. When Amy's Baking Company appeared on Kitchen Nightmares in 2013, they received a lot of negative press over the way they interacted with customers and Gordon Ramsay.

Due to their antics, they became the first and only restaurant in the series where Ramsay walked away from. Naturally this opened to a lot more bashing from people online and more news articles regarding the restaurant.

Unfortunately, the couple that owned that restaurant decided to double down on the negativity by harshly responding to critics on their Facebook page and behaving erratically on TV.

This started a downward spiral where negative press resulted in more bizarre antics which further generated negative press. Ultimately, the couple's reputation were in tatters and the restaurant had to be closed.

5. *Establishing Authority*

Even if a journalist has done all their research with regards to a certain topic, they still would welcome the input of an expert in that field. This is why they often ask local businesses for opinions on certain matters.

For instance, if a reporter comes to you for your opinion on the local economy and you give an impression that you know how things work, you help the journalist finish their article while also establishing yourself as an authority on the matter.

However, what you must remember is that the information you are going to provide is only going to help you if it can capture the attention of the audience. For instance, backing your opinions with hard data and making sure that your information is correct will make you sound even more credible.

If done properly, your opinion as shown on that article will increase your brand's visibility on social media and funnel enough traffic to your web pages.

The Art of Using Press Releases

The Press Release might look like this remnant of a bygone era in PR. In actuality, it is a rather effective tool for marketing, especially through social media.

However, in order to really make full use of press releases in the Internet Age, you have to understand that there have been considerable changes in the concept. Here are some of them:

1. *Search Engine Visibility*

To start things off, you have to understand that search engine bots now can differentiate between promotional, educational, and news-related content. This can mean two things. For audiences, they can discern whether or not that content was published to either provide information or promote a certain brand.

For marketers, this allows you to monitor what type of content your target audiences will resonate with the most.

One telltale sign that your PR in social media is effective is if the search engines feature your press releases first, followed by your social media content, and then your main web pages. Not only does this mean that your presence in the search engines is quite strong, this allows your audiences to quickly go through whatever content you put out there.

2. *The Narrative*

Of course, press releases should tell a story. However, they also need to provide continuity and this is where a lot of brands fail when making press releases on social media.

Think of it this way: If the movie that Disney released after *Black Panther* is *Avengers: Endgame* instead of *Infinity War*, and you are wondering why they are leapfrogging through time to save their dead friends, the first question you'd be asking is "What happened in between?!"

This is the same for press releases. In essence, a press release should be an opportunity for you to showcase to your audience how your company has grown through the years.

For example, if one press release talks about you breaking into the market, then the next press release should cover what you have achieved since then. And the press release after that would be your company appearing in big trade shows, collaborating with other businesses, and showing off new products.

By making your stories follow a coherent narrative, you give the impression to potential customers (and investors) that you have something potentially groundbreaking in your business and it would be wise for them to start dealing with you now. Without that narrative, all your press releases would sound like boring updates to your company.

3. *Frequency*

One question often asked is "How often should one publish a press release?" There is actually no formula for press release frequency but it is recommended that the gap between your press releases span only months, not years.

If you are going to publish a press release in August of 2019, then maybe the next one would be in November of the same year, or January 2020.

On the other hand, it is not recommended that you put out press releases every week. Social media algorithms often regard that as spam, as not a lot of companies have newsworthy content to share on a weekly basis.

As such, a good pace for your press releases would either be once a month or once every quarter.

4. *Finding Leverage*

Timing is also crucial for your press releases. If possible, make one before you take part in a major event. And, if you are the first brand to talk about that upcoming event, you can funnel a lot of traffic to your web pages as people follow you for blow-by-blow coverage.

Also, being one of the first businesses to be quoted by a third-party article gives the impression to audiences that your brand has some clout. This could increase interest for your brand which naturally leads to an increase in site traffic.

5. *Content Marketing*

Your press releases should be incorporated into your content marketing strategies for all your social media profiles. You can do this by actually dedicating a slot for them in your content creation schedule and assigning writers who are proficient with journalistic-style writing.

With this, your staff can devote a portion of their time creating your press releases as opposed to it being an afterthought. And the less forced your press release sounds like, the more effective it is in creating a narrative that your audience can follow.

Lastly, this gives your staff an opportunity to master the art of creating a press release. Not every press release you put out has to only tell your readers that your company has grown considerably in the past few months.

More often than not, it gives your staff an opportunity to look back and take note of how the content they are producing has changed in quality over time. Your staff might be surprised as to how their content has changed in tone and style through the years.

Dealing with Online Backlash

Although you can do your best to remain on everybody's good side, there is still the chance that you will find yourself in a rather tricky situation with social media. It's expected that you will make mistakes on your social media campaigns along the way, but the bigger problem is if that mistake generates a lot of negative publicity.

Fortunately, there is a way for you to weather through the negative press and come out with your dignity intact. And to do that, there are a few tips to remember.

A. *Be The First to Know*

Set up alerts and notifications on your social media pages to know if negative press is building up on you. Your social media team should make it a habit to periodically scan your channels to see if a person has any issue with your business. Legitimate or otherwise.

You can also use Google alerts and other similar apps to notify your team in case any mention of you is made is made by a third-party entity.

B. *React Quickly*

Customers use social media to complain, as this is the fastest way they can get attention to their grievances. If you know something is raised up against you, be the first to respond and find a way to address that situation with the person to the best of your ability.

If a lot of people have already seen that negative comment, the best that you can do is to address the situation publicly by issuing a statement.

The worst that you can do is to delete those comments as people can track if any omission has been made on your part. Treat a complaint as an opportunity to do the right thing and solve the problem effectively.

C. *Make Yourself Accountable*

In a case when you did make an honest mistake, the best thing that you can do is to own up to it. A humble response to a criticism gives the impression that you value the opinion of those that have been loyally consuming your products and services.

One good example of this is YouTube celebrity Jojo Siwa. When her products were discovered to have harmful substances in them, she was the first to apologize and promised to revamp the standards in her products. She even promised refunds for anyone who has already purchased her product.

D. *Actually Fix the Problem*

The most important thing that you can do when dealing with online backlash is to actually address the situation presented.

This is the most labor-intensive part of the process, as you will have to look up where you made the mistake and how you can avoid similar instances from occurring in the future.

If the problem stems from issues in your product, the most obvious solution is to recall your products and investigate where things went wrong in production. If the problem is a tweet or status update you made, the best that you can do is to order a redaction or issue a formal apology.

Whatever the problem, the responsibility of fixing always lies with your business.

To Conclude

Without a doubt, handling the PR for your brand in the age of social media can be demanding. Do it wrong and you open your brand up to a lot of negative backlash.

However, that is not to say that public relations will remain a difficult aspect to handle in your business. All that is required of you is to keep track of what has changed and to always find a way to keep your audience interested in the story behind your business.

Chapter 9: Social Media Success Stories: Organic and Paid Marketing Strategies that Work

After all is said and done, the one thing that you would want to ask would most likely be this:

Will all of these strategies work for me?

There is no definitive answer to that, as only you can determine what strategies will work the best for your business. However, that is not to say that some companies have not managed to use marketing strategies to gain a foothold in the social media arena.

In fact, there are quite a lot of brands and people out there that managed to make their marketing strategies work for them. And to give you just a bit of inspiration for your upcoming campaigns, here are their stories.

I. *Facebook Promo*

This paid marketing campaign follows the typical conversion goals, specifically encouraging their audiences to sign up for a trial for a series of Internet marketing lessons.

But, instead of merely settling for the usual text ad with a CTA, Promo decided to produce a ten-second video with a baby dancing on an open track next to a boom box.

123

As of 2019, Promo's campaign has reached 2.2 million views, 4.2 thousand reactions, more than 590 comments, and 500 shares. And aside from an increase in engagement on their Facebook profile, Promo also saw an increase in their click-through rates by 42% and a decrease in their cost per action by 28%.

Why Promo's ad worked is quite simple. First, it targeted a very specific demographic: people running small businesses. Second, it laid out the problem and the solution in one paragraph so people don't have to overthink and overanalyze.

And lastly, it used an eye-catching video to get people to click through.

MobileMonkey

Facebook's Messenger feature has become a semi-platform for marketing in 2018 and this campaign proves just that. MobileMonkey's campaign in 2018 was optimized for the Messenger app in the sense that clicking it would direct you to a chatbot.

But marketing a chatbot conventionally is not exactly appealing so MobileMonkey had to find a way to get everybody's attention first. How they did that was through a shockingly unusual image of a multicolored mechanical unicorn. It's enough to make everyone do a double take on their news feed just to process the imagery.

But MobileMonkey's cleverness did not stop there. Their CTA just says "Type: Send Me the Secrets." It's direct enough to tell people what to do but is vague enough to not spoil whatever offer MobileMonkey has in store for those that clicked through.

This is one great example of gamification where you make your content highly engaging by offering something tangible as an incentive for those that follow your commands.

And how did this campaign helped MobileMonkey? Its engagement was quite high that the company's cost per lead for this campaign was a measly $5.00. That's thirty times less than what they used to spend for their ads in the past.

Grammarly

One problem that has often plagued advertisers is getting their message across to their audience without becoming spam. Grammarly managed to do just that with their organic advertising campaign way back in 2018.

The goal of the campaign was very simple: to do branding. But Grammarly told a rather relatable story in a two-minute video that ended with a rather compelling message: Write the Future.

Storytelling works great in selling a product or service, especially if the thing that you are selling feels complementary to the story itself. In Grammarly's case, the ad did not shove their service right at the forefront but included it in the story in a manner that is natural and non-intrusive to the theme of the narrative.

And, aside from a compelling CTA, Grammarly also added an element of social proof as they linked a *Forbes* article mentioning them in the video's description.

Needless to say, the campaign reached more than 5 million people with their cost per click reduced to roughly $0.50 per complete views. It also is important to note that Grammarly's cost per million for this ad was 76% cheaper than their usual ads.

Airbnb

What is the best way to promote yourself while also building rapport with your customer base? Use their experiences as the core of your advertising, of course.

Airbnb's marketing on Facebook is reliant on the content generated by their satisfied customers. Simply put, the company uses photos of exotic locations that their customers have taken, which they would otherwise have not enjoyed were it not for Airbnb's services.

What you have to remember is that the algorithm used on Facebook actually favors visual content over hard linking. As such, any marketing campaign that takes advantage of visual media is expected to reach a lot of people organically there.

In 2018 alone, Airbnb managed to triple their return of investment while also lowering their ad's CPA rates by 47%.

Toyota

Being authentic and having a strong connection with your user base tends to make any ad campaign more effective and Toyota's "Feeling the Street" campaign is proof of that.

This ad is a cross-platform contest wherein Toyota would use images generated from street musicians in Instagram and Twitter for a series of visual ads on Facebook.

By showing the culture that their products can live in, Toyota managed to make the central focus of their ads more of the people that can use their product than their actual products.

As a result, Toyota's Feeling the Street campaign managed to generate 1.2 million engagements in 2018 alone. That is a 440% increase in engagements over their ad campaigns in the year before that.

II. *Twitter*

Netflix

Technically speaking, Netflix is not marketing their services or shows on Twitter. But that hasn't stopped their Twitter handle from being one of the most visited and engaged channels on the site today.

This is because Netflix does not market itself conventionally through Twitter. Instead, it uses its handle there to celebrate pop culture and the Internet community.

Aside from the usual updates and retweets, Netflix's Twitter profile is almost dedicated to sharing memes and pop culture references. And, if you are well versed in millennial humor, you would know that those two things resonate with younger folks a lot.

One lesson to be drawn here is to never underestimate entertainment values for your content. Any profile that can speak the language of Internet users and generate content that celebrates online culture is bound to make itself popular on any platform it markets on.

Oberlo

This B2B company caters to small businesses and rookie entrepreneurs. And, given that rather small reach, you'd expect for Oberlo's Twitter marketing to be rather generic and uninspired.

However, a look at Oberlo's Twitter handle would prove that it is anything but those two. Its content is filled with motivational quotes and soothing images that one tends to expect from a life improvement coach or philosopher.

The reason for Oberlo's Twitter campaign is to give its audience a healthy mix of motivation and information. And anyone who is still trying to break into the market knows how important those two things are.

So, by tapping into needs that their audiences can relate to, Oberlo managed to generate a strong following on Twitter.

And most of these leads have actually converted into customers.

PlayStation UK

A reactive content strategy is where one adapts to the language and culture of the platform. And in Twitter, one can easily find themselves in the middle of a cultural shift.

PlayStation UK understands this and thus constantly provides content that reflects changes in Internet culture. For instance, if a new form of meme pops up, this handle would then mold their messaging to fit the format of that meme or, at the very least, give a nod to it.

And the best part about this is that PlayStation UK manages to constantly remold their advertising to adapt while still following Twitter's character limits.

Wendy's

When it comes to humor, no other Twitter handle could match the biting sarcasm of Wendy's. In fact, the content found on the profile is a mixture of the usual company update and the profile engaging in Twitter "beefs" with other people, or roasting other competitors like McDonald's.

As of now, the growth of Wendy's Twitter handle in terms of popularity is quite baffling. Perhaps it could be traced back to the fact that Internet humor is quite unpredictable. If you force yourself to be funny online, it wouldn't generate as much interest. But whoever is in charge of Wendy's profile knows when and how to drop a one-liner.

Or perhaps it could be traced back to the fact that the profile, though rather scathing with its remarks, tends to hold back on the more offensive stuff. This way, it keeps a certain level of goodwill with its target audience without becoming needlessly abrasive.

What could not be denied, however, is the fact that Wendy's Twitter profile has more than 970,000 new followers as of 2018, many of which are awaiting which hapless fast food chain Twitter profile it is going to start a tussle with next.

Casper

Cross-platform marketing is something that is highly recommended these days since it consolidates all the traffic coming through your different social media channels. Casper is one company that does this but takes things even further by linking their Twitter handle on popular platforms.

In a bid to help people sleep, Casper created the Casper Sleep Channel which can be found on YouTube, Spotify, and IGTV. They would then provide teasers and updates of whatever content they have produced on these channels on their Twitter along with their Facebook and Instagram handles.

The only draw here is that Casper is now spending more just to keep multiple social media fronts active. However, this does pay in dividends as the following for their brand has significantly increased across all platforms, which easily translates into increased profits.

Google Maps

Being a highly visual app, it is expected for Google Maps to use a highly visual approach for their marketing on Twitter. But how does Google Maps exactly make its handle there stand out from the competition?

First, there is consistency. When Maps would announce changes in the app, their next tweet would be designed in such a way that it looked like a smartphone app but with the changes in Google Maps highlighted there.

What makes this strategy effective is in its simplicity. Using the most basic of tools on Twitter, Google managed to convey their message across despite the platform's inherent limitations.

The other factor is their ability to provide additional content despite the word limit on Twitter. Whenever they provide an update, Google Maps will also include a link where their audience can find a better explanation of the changes. And if the link does not suffice, Google will always place a GIF or a video in their updates.

This way, Google Maps managed to catch the attention of people who are looking for an in-depth explanation of their changes or are content enough with the basic announcement.

Lastly, Google keeps things fun and exciting. For instance, if their announcement falls on a quirky holiday like, say,

Spaghetti Day, Google will make a quick reference to the celebration in their tweet.

It's practically a situation where everybody wins. On one hand, Google manages to inform their audience about the changes in their Maps app to the best of their ability. On the other hand, they keep their audience engaged by presenting such important information in a way that is interesting and funny.

III. *YouTube*

Reebok

In conjunction with their #HonorYourDays campaign, Reebok released a video called 25,915 days. It featured the life of a woman in reverse as she ran a Spartan Race (with Reebok shoes, of course) to the day that she was born.

The message of the video was quite simple. The average human being lives for an average of 25,915 days and one must use those days to push their body to the limit.

And just like any good video campaign, the main product serves only to complement the story, not steal the spotlight from a rather moving narrative. And, to top it off, it ends with a strong CTA with the words "Calculate Your Days."

What makes Reebok's ad work is that it creates a sense of urgency without making things bleak. And urgency is a particularly strong motivator which makes any message you convey all the more actionable and compelling.

GoPro

Not every marketing campaign you create for YouTube has to directly relate to your brand or your products/services, and GoPro's "Fireman Saves a Kitty" video is proof of just that.

The premise of the video is quite simple. It just shows a random firefighter saving a kitten from a burning building. What makes it unique is that GoPro is never one to show modern day heroism, as their brand is more about adventures and extreme sports.

However, it did prove to be one of the company's most successful and engaging YouTube videos to date. The only takeaway from this campaign is that one must never hesitate to explore the different facets of their brand's image.

By showcasing the work of a firefighter, GoPro is subtly implying that there are other thrills found out there and ones that can actually inspire and uplift.

Plus, it also helps that it showcases a cat and it's an open secret that almost everybody on the Internet loves cats.

Coachella

It's typical for big events to be advertised on YouTube. But what if that actual event would not only be advertised there but also broadcasted?

This is what the organizers of Coachella did when they decided to stream the entire event Live on YouTube. For several days straight, viewers could see the performances in the music festival at the comfort of their own homes, and practically for free.

The end result? Coachella's first ever livestream on YouTube garnered 4 million views and the numbers have only risen in the years that followed.

Old Spice

When targeting two different demographics for the same line of products, it would be best that you convey the same message differently.

Old Spice did this when they marketed their line of products to adult males with the "The Man Your Man Could Smell Like" campaign, featuring Isaiah Mustafa encouraging ladies to make the man in their life use the company's body wash.

Needless to say, the campaign became one of Old Spice's most successful commercials in the 2000s which gave rise to other campaigns featuring Mustafa and his sultry voice.

By the 2010s, however, Old Spice decided to target younger male demographics. And to do that, they came up with the "Smells Like Power" campaign featuring Terry Crews in a series of insane, reality-bending advertisements. It was bright, loud, and weird and each 30-second video would net in views by the millions after publishing.

In 2015, everything came to a head when Old Spice decided to feature both stars in a crossover campaign called "Make a Smellmitment" which advertised the Timber and Bear Glove scents.

134

Featuring a clash between the sophistication of the Mustafa campaign and insanity of the Crews campaign, the campaign also became Old Spice's most successful advertisement for the latter half of the decade.

Sephora

In these days, telling your audience why your brand is the best is no longer enough. You also have to show them how your products and offerings can be applied in real world situations.

In Sephora's case, their YouTube channel does not only feature the usual product promotions but also step-by-step tutorials on how to achieve certain makeup effects using their products.

Then, to generate traffic to their web page, which leads to sales, Sephora includes links to their website in the description for each video.

The main takeaway from Sephora's strategy is that if you insist on highlighting your products for your campaigns, you have to make sure that they are presented in a manner that makes them relevant to the message that you are trying to convey.

And, of course, never forget to make sure that the video actually generates enough traffic to your main pages. This can be done with the help of a strong CTA partnered with a working link to your sales page.

Adidas

One great way to market yourself in social media is if you allow your brand to become an opportunity for the public to directly interact with celebrities and influential people. In 2014, during the FIFA World Cup, Adidas published a series of videos called The Dugout which was a series of interviews with popular football players, managers, and other influential people in the industry.

Here, and for the first time in the history of the World Cup, people had the opportunity to have their questions answered by stars like Luca Moura and have them directly answered in a virtual press conference of sorts.

The Dugout became one of Adidas' most successful video campaigns to date, with more than 1.5 million views on the platform and with an increase in subscriptions to the channel by 300%.

IV. Instagram

ESPN

News programs often have it hard on Twitter. It is as if the constant stream of news is turning people off which leads to fewer engagements the more frequent a news handle posts there.

Back then, ESPN used to get in between 300 to 3,000 comments for their posts but this all changed when they started using polls for their Instagram posts.

The strategy is quite simple: ESPN asks a question with several different answers. Of course, sports fans would not only pick any of the questions but would defend their answer in the comments with their opinions.

No matter how polarizing an issue gets, the engagement ESPN receives from their online quizzes is quite considerable with comments going well beyond the 30,000 mark and more than 1,000 shares.

The lesson here is to find ways to make your audience interact with you. Polls and online questions can often do this because they require answers. And answers start a conversation, which increases engagement for your content.

Lego

What if your company is in the middle of a rather uneventful stretch? What if the industry you are part of has no major events or issues that need tackling? What if everybody's attention is on another event/issue happening in another part of the world?

Lego's answer to that on Instagram is quite simple: Jump on the bandwagon.

For instance, when everybody was focused on the Royal Wedding in May 2018, Lego published a picture depicting the couple made from Lego blocks and with the trending #RoyalWedding hashtag.

The end result is the picture garnering Lego more than 300 comments and well over 100,000 views.

Why this worked is quite simple. Events trend in the online world because people are interested in whatever has happened or is going to happen. You can take advantage of this brief shift of focus in the online community by showing the rest of the world that you know what's trending.

The thing with Lego is that it has a rather malleable image due to its products. Basically, since everyone can create anything with pieces of Lego, the company can also market itself in almost every known event happening across the world right now.

Casper

Pillows and contests sound like two things that don't go hand in hand but Casper managed to find a way to bring these two things together. Wanting to reach out to a lot of people, Casper launched an interactive campaign which is best described as an online pillow fight.

The premise is simple: On a website they set up, users can hit each other with an online pillow. They would then promote the pillow fight on Instagram using videos showing the online fight.

The result, obviously, was that people started tagging their friends to come to the website to have their pillow fight. The more long-term result was that Casper retargeted their old customers while bringing in droves of new ones who have become aware of their line of pillows and mattresses.

What lesson that could be drawn from here is that there is absolutely no limit as to how you can market your products in any platform that you operate on. In Casper's case, they turned a sleeping accessory into a tool where people can interact with each other through the Internet.

By keeping your campaigns interesting, you are bound to keep your brand relevant and more people will become aware of it. And with an increase in brand awareness comes multiple opportunities to convert your audience into loyal customers.

Rent The Runway

Picture this scenario: Your company is going to launch an update to your app. Naturally, app updates are boring content since they contain mostly technical stuff.

So, how are you going to market it? By making it look like the app was in response to customer comments.

Rent The Runway did this when they announced a new update for their app which allows people to see whether or not the clothes they are about to purchase has pockets.

Naturally, this announcement would not generate much buzz among fashionistas but, luckily enough, Rent the Runway has a picture of a comment from one of their customers asking if pockets can be one of the filters for their app.

And so Rent the Runway posted their announcement with a screenshot of the comment, explaining in the caption how they came to the decision to add that feature. And, soon enough, the announcement would manage to net 10,000 likes.

Using feedback generated by your customers is not only a creative way of selling your products or announcing changes in your services. It's one way of subtly saying that you do care for their needs. By giving the impression that you are interested in providing what the people need, you naturally endear yourself to the public.

Citrix

Marketing on a highly visual platform can be difficult if the product you are selling is highly technical. This is the problem faced by Citrix, a company that provides remote device access services to their customers.

Their product is targeted towards people who are interested in cloud-based storage and data protection, which is the demographic that is not as prominent in Instagram when compared to other platforms.

Their creative workaround to this problem? Wordplay. Simply put, Citrix's promoted their app by linking it to an issue that almost every adult can relate to: a cluttered physical workspace.

So, by making people understand that their app is to online databases what sorting and cleaning is to physical work spaces, Citrix bridged the gap between them and their customers, resulting in tons of engagement on their page.

When having to market a fairly complicated and technical product/service, it is necessary to keep things simple and relatable. Find a way to make the crux of the problem your marketing is trying to solve into something that people can instantly understand.

Whether it is a mundane walk to the business or having to file taxes, there are quite a lot of situations out there that can be analogous to the problems your products are trying to solve. Finding that link and marketing your brand in a highly visual platform should be easy.

Conclusion

After everything has been said and done, there is still one question that you need to answer:

What is the ultimate measure of success for your social media campaigns?

Some would say it is the increase in your brand's awareness. The instant that more people know about you compared to a few months ago, then your social media campaign is a success.

Others would say it is the increase in web traffic. Granted, all the strategies that you have read in this book have been designed to funnel and consolidate all traffic coming from your social media pages to your main web pages.

And then there are others who would claim that it is the increase in engagement in your content. This could hold some truth, as an increase in activity on your social media pages is a telltale sign that there is considerable interest in your brand. And where interest lies, profit will soon follow.

Then there are people who say that it is in the discovery of new segments in the market. This is a sign that your products and services can actually be made to fulfill needs that you haven't thought of before. And, of course, knowing that other demographics like your brand is a sign that your range of influence in the field of social media has expanded.

The truth, however, is that all of these metrics are all telling that your marketing campaigns are working. However, there is one other factor that trumps them all: conversion.

Conversion begins when a person becomes so interested that they visit your channels and are convinced by what you are offering. This interest is then followed by a willingness to visit your sales page or your physical business.

Once there, they will then be convinced enough to start a transaction with your business and part with their hard-earned money in return for what you are offering.

If they find value in what you are offering and would want to consume more of it, then and only then can you declare that all your marketing campaigns have been effective.

Sure, marketing in a field that is as dynamic and fickle as social media has its ups and downs. Even the best-laid plans that you have designed can be derailed by a single misfire.

However, the beauty with marketing is that there is always room for improvement. If you do fail, there is that chance to learn from where you messed up and start all over again.

The risk of stepping out of your comfort zone in the hopes of offering something that people will find value in does reap some rewards. And you will know that your efforts did pay off when your brand's name alone is enough to convince people to start doing business with you.

I would like to thank you and congratulate you for finishing this book!

I hope all that you learned here will help you in making your business stand out from your competition in the world of social media.

The next step here is to actually implement whatever strategies you have thought of and measure your success.

I wish you the best of luck!

Thank you

Before you go, I just wanted to say thank you for purchasing my book.

You could have picked from dozens of other books on the same topic but you took a chance and chose this one.

So, a HUGE thanks to you for getting this book and for reading all the way to the end.

Now I wanted to ask you for a small favor. **Could you please consider posting a review on the platform? Reviews are one of the easiest ways to support the work of independent authors.**

This feedback will help me continue to write the type of books that will help you get the results you want. So if you enjoyed it, please let me know!

Lastly, don't forget to grab a copy of your Free Bonuses *"The Fastest Way to Make Money with Affiliate Marketing"* and *"Top 10 Affiliate Offers to Promote"*
.

Just go to the link below.

https://theartofmastery.com/chandler-free-gift

www.ingramcontent.com/pod-product-compliance
Lightning Source LLC
Chambersburg PA
CBHW071424210326

41597CB00020B/3645